This Splendid Journey

Joel Nederhood

CRC Publications
Grand Rapids, Michigan

P&R Publishing
Phillipsburg, New Jersey

Scripture quotations in this publication are from the HOLY BIBLE, NEW INTERNATIONAL VERSION, © 1973, 1978, 1984, International Bible Society. Used by permission of Zondervan Bible Publishers.

Copublished by CRC Publications, 2850 Kalamazoo Ave. SE, Grand Rapids, MI 49560, 1-800-333-8300, and P&R Publishing, P.O. Box 817, Phillipsburg, NJ 08865, 1-800-631-0094.

Cover photo: SuperStock.

Library of Congress Cataloging-in-Publication Data

Nederhood, Joel H.
    This splendid journey / by Joel Nederhood.
       p.   cm.
    ISBN 1-56212-359-9 (CRC), 0-87552-364-1 (P&R)
    1. Meditations. I. Title.
  BV4832.2.N35   1998
  242—dc21   98-28950
                                                        CIP

10 9 8 7 6 5 4 3 2

Acknowledgments

To be a Christian is to be part of a body of believers.

I think of the body of people who make my life what it is. Mary Lou, my wife and faith-sister—this is actually her book as well as mine, for our "twoness" has long been gone, replaced by the "oneness" of the marriage mystery. As I grow older, I find myself becoming more like my father—following his often solitary path of exploration in the Scripture; his presence still broods in my life. And my mother, still there to comment on the wonderment of children; it was she who planted the first seeds of faith in my toddler heart. My siblings, scattered across the continent (what is it that will not allow us to live close to one another?)—each of them is a unique and fascinating person who has contributed to my sense of life's richness and grace. And my own children—Maria, Carol, and David—each a special gift, each different from the other and from my wife and me—how impoverished our life would be without them!

I think of the body at Bethel, the believers who over the years have always been there to help in bitter times and jubilant. One of them, Bill Schipper, has provided invaluable help over the decades; lover of books, lover of the church, lover of Christ—frequently he brought me just the article or publication I needed. And there is the broader church that has given me so much. Few ministries could be more privileged and exciting than the one entrusted to me. And there have been those who have helped with these very pages: Paul Faber, with whom I worked for many years in the publication of *Today (The Family Altar)*, and Ruth Vander Hart and Bob De Moor, who encouraged me to write *This Splendid Journey.*

Along with my overwhelming debt to God, I owe a debt to such as these. My gratitude to each and all of them.

Contents

Preface

It has been a great delight to write the pages that follow, but there have been times of doubt while doing so. The writing has spanned many months, and during those months there have been times when experiences have tended to mock the very idea that life is splendid.

Even as I write this brief preface, I am challenged to think deeply about two heartrending events. The toddler grandson of a dear friend has gone to be with Christ, crushed beneath the wheels of his father's pickup. What agony! And I have learned that a friend is gradually being robbed of strength as Lou Gehrig's disease works its relentless way within him. If only these were rare events, but they are not.

We all have our own private collections of disappointment, terror, pain, and anguish. Yet, to be a Christian is to declare, in the face of all this, that life is truly splendid. We have to admit that if we had to depend on empirical evidence to support this declaration, we would finally be confused and embarrassed. But this is a faith declaration.

Faith is a unique vision. It is focused on God. And that means it is focused specifically on God's Word to us in the Bible. The following readings, then, are about God's Word. They are a type of devotional reading, but I do not consider them devotional in the conventional sense. I think of them as treatments—reactions to the Bible from out of life's experience. The last few lines of each reading are more prayerful than the rest, but in a sense the whole treatment is a kind of prayer. The "Amen" at the end of each one goes with all that comes before it.

I have tried to be truthful in these readings—to be honest. This may seem strange to say, but it's not always easy for those of us who have studied some theology and have worked at a church-assigned task to be honest. I have written these reactions because I have wanted to, and they come from a variety of experiences, so they may lack some coherence—that is, one may not follow directly from the other. But they are a part of my testimony after having read the Bible for many years. *Lord, this is what your Word has meant to me, and I realize I have much more to learn about it.*

There is nothing in writing more important than God's Word. There is nothing more beautiful, and there is nothing more humbling. Nothing. We can spend our entire life reading the Bible, studying it, and thinking about it, and still we will sense that we have not succeeded in capturing its fullness. There is always more.

And the one thing about it that I wish to stress here is that the Bible is a revelation not only of God and his love but also of who we are and of how splendid our lives actually are. Our lives are God's poetry. We live them in the vestibule of eternity, and what we do and how we think contribute in some mysterious way to our eternal treasure in Christ. This is true because of grace, grace alone.

"God is so good, he's so good to me."

Joel Nederhood
June 1998

This Splendid Journey

God . . . predestined [us] to be conformed to [Christ's] likeness. . . .

Romans 8:29

The sentence just before the one we are looking at today is well known among longtime Christians. Sometimes they simply give the reference—Romans 8:28—and that is enough. Anyone familiar with the passage knows just what they're talking about: *All things work together for good.*

But sometimes that declaration is made between clenched teeth by those who are touching the depth of unexplained suffering and who have long considered themselves Christians. There's a supreme irony in tragedy that has no explanation and leads to no foreseeable good. Romans 8:28. Come now, is the Bible serious when it declares without qualification that "in all things God works for the good of those who love him . . ."?

There is ample reason to question this statement if it stands all by itself. It makes sense only when seen as a certainty that flows from our knowledge of the magnificent process described in the two sentences that follow it: "For those God foreknew he also predestined to be conformed to the likeness of his Son, that he might be the firstborn among many brothers. And those he predestined, he also called; those he called, he also justified; those he justified, he also glorified" (8:29-30).

I talked with a friend of mine about this passage a few days before writing this meditation, and we marveled at the splendid sweep described here, from the beginning of a person in the mind of God to the ultimate glorification by which that person would end up looking like Jesus.

My friend was dying at the time. In fact, I was too. But in his case it was quite obvious, and the cancer that had invaded his body was what got us talking about what our lives were all about. I was dying in the more general sense in which all of us are. He happened to be a preacher—but preachers, in case you don't know, are as puzzled and stricken as anybody else when they find themselves looking at their own death. So we began to talk not just about Romans 8:28 but also about verses 29 and 30 as well—and it's those last two verses that make the first one make sense.

Isn't it a splendid journey that we find described here? To be sure, the path we travel along the way is strewn with horrible realities and inexplicable tragedies. But not always, of course. Let's not make it worse than it is. Thank God there are times of indescribable ecstasy. But there are enough pathetic events that occur—and if not in our own lives, then surely in the lives of those so close to us that their suffering becomes our own—to make us question what God is up to. There is so much in life that makes no sense in itself. And our very ecstasies are mocked by the cruelties that make our poor bodies pitiable.

So we handle Romans 8:28 in our misery and shake our heads in confusion. And then we read on and discover that nothing in our present circumstances may be allowed to obscure the splendor of our journey from beginning in God's mind to someday being like him.

Predestination is a word that often incites ridicule and invites disbelief. It can do that when it operates only in the realm of formal theologies. But when it is connected to our life's splendid journey as we discover it in the sentences that follow Romans 8:28, it becomes indescribably wonderful. Predestination is the beginning in eternity of believers who are carried through their various life experiences toward glory. And when we talk about *glory,* we are talking about the dazzling purity and perfection of God. Someday the glory of God's purity will be so shared with God's people that they will be like Jesus, perfect human beings as God intends them to be.

This means, doesn't it, that no life experience we have is accidental and meaningless. It means that every life experience is carefully selected by the God who has predestined us. Every life experience contributes to our becoming more Christlike. Our call to faith, our faith itself, even justification—all of it has but one goal: glorification.

As my friend and I embraced in parting, just hours before he died, we both realized that the sickroom in which he lay was the vestibule of glory.

Look in your mercy, dear God, upon your dying children. Help all of us to see our life experiences as events you have designed to bring us into the glorious place where you are. Forgive us, O God, for so often not looking like Christ. Comfort us with the certainty that everything that happens to us is for our good. In Christ, Amen.

Meditation 2

The Birthday Psalm

LORD . . . *you know me.*

Psalm 139:1

Birthdays are exciting when you are a child, but as the years roll along, birthdays also become occasions for wonderment. Who am I anyway? What am I doing in this world? Why am I me? Why am I the way I am? Why did I experience the things I experienced over the years? These are long, far-reaching thoughts—puzzling questions. And as the years wind down, you wonder when and how it's all going to end. And what's beyond?

When the long thoughts come, it's good to read Psalm 139, because it connects our lives to God. From this psalm there comes this astonishing fact: "Lord, you know me." Start with that, and let it be the foundation on which to build a bit of biblical self-esteem, which is different from the kind by which we seek to convince ourselves we are important when so much else says we're not. The Bible says that God knows me—and in the Bible that word *knows* has overtones of intimacy. God doesn't just know me as a line item on a printout; he knows me better than I know myself. He knows my thoughts, and he knows the words I speak even before I do.

This psalm also tells me that I live my earthly years in the presence of God, in God's company. "Such knowledge is too wonderful for me" (139:6). Believers in Christ can read this psalm and meditate on the reality of God's companionship. For those who are older, veterans of foreign wars and of countless other dangers, it is marvelous to contemplate the way God is always there—even when you make your bed in the depths or fly off into the dawn or sail to the far side of the sea.

God is like a father who teases his little child by moving back and forth so that his little one cannot get by. The child moves to the right, and the father moves to block him. The child moves to the left, and he's blocked again. Finally the child looks up into the father's eyes, puzzled, and the father laughs and lets him pass. God never lets us pass. We encounter him every time we make a move.

The Lord knows me—Psalm 139 makes this point relentlessly. We are invited to examine the mysterious days before our birth when events occurred in our mothers' wombs that still bear upon our capacities and our emotions. Long before ultrasound, the ancients spoke of the divine weaver in the womb. There, in the womb, the code was put in place that now governs each day.

O Lord, you know me—how is this possible? When we are children and our mothers have birthday parties for us, we feel like the king of the mountain. When all our friends come over and there's a cake and gifts and games, we figure the whole world is paying attention. Later we discover that we are not kings or queens at all; in fact, we discover there isn't even any mountain. We look around and see literally billions of people, and though we may have managed to build a little empire for ourselves, it is infinitesimally small and so are we. How can God know me?

It's interesting that Psalm 139 does not speak of God's knowledge of his people simplistically. Here we find a recognition of the fact that this can be true only if God has an infinite capacity for knowledge. "How precious to me are your thoughts, O God! How vast is the sum of them! Were I to count them, they would outnumber the grains of sand" (139:17-18).

If we think about our lives without reference to this omniscient, omnipotent, omnipresent God, they are empty and disappointing. But when our God is the omni-God of Psalm 139, we may believe that our poor, faltering lives have their own special place in God's great scheme of things. Faith is the key to all this. Through faith in Jesus Christ I may believe that what Psalm 139 says is true.

The Lord knows me—what good news! The Lord who knows me loves me—what good news! The Lord who knows and loves me has made me what I am, and I can never escape him—what good news! There is no better news for birthday boys and birthday girls, whatever their age.

On our birthdays, O Lord, help us to ponder Psalm 139. Ah, yes, it is true: your thoughts are more in number than the grains of sand on the seashore; they are in fact more than everything in the entire universe. Help us to believe you are great enough to know each of us individually and that you care for us in your love and grace. For Jesus' sake, Amen.

Jealousy

"The LORD, whose name is Jealous, is a jealous God."
Exodus 34:14

Jealousy gets a bad press. We automatically consider it reprehensible and evil. "Why, I do believe you're jealous," a wife may say to her husband when he complains because she has had lunch with a male colleague from the office. Her tone of voice implies, "Clarence, don't be so foolish and childish." He may have replied, "You're absolutely right—I'm jealous."

Of course, there's a form of jealousy called *envy,* which is sick. It afflicts little girls and teenage boys, office workers and retired folk—people of all kinds. Envy crucified Jesus (Matt. 27:18).

But God's jealousy is good, and it is so much a part of his being that he wants to be known as a jealous God. Many of us have noticed the declaration of God's jealousy in the second commandment, in which God explained to his trembling people that they should not make any idols because he was jealous and would destroy the people if they did.

Jealousy is so fully connected with God's divine being that he wants us, at least occasionally, to address him with this name. The sentence we are focusing on here is startling and absolute. The word for "jealous" is *qanna,* and in Exodus 34 God tells Moses his name is *God the Jealous God.*

If you read Exodus, you learn that the same people who received God's commandments in a firestorm at Sinai disobeyed these commandments even before they left the mountain. Within days after hearing God's prohibition about making idols, the man destined to be the high priest, Aaron, fashioned a golden calf, and the people worshiped it with their lewd play. The God whose name is Jealous responded with deadly punishment.

So it is that in Exodus 34 this God, who had been so treacherously betrayed by the people he had saved from slavery, reiterates and underscores the fact that jealousy is his very name and that he will not share his honor with anyone or anything. Talk about timely reminders—we certainly need to hear Exodus 34:14 again.

There is no reason to believe that God is more tolerant now than he was when he spoke to Israel. If you listen to what people say today about religion and spirituality and about God, you would think that somewhere along the line God was converted, just as people are converted. Whereas he used to be pretty hard to get along with, now it seems that God is willing to recognize a little bit of good in all kinds of religion.

One of the earliest heresies to afflict the Christian church, promoted by a shipbuilder named Marcion, proclaimed that there is a vast difference between the God of the Old Testament and the God of the New. Marcion said that the God of the New Testament was much kinder than the God of the Old Testament. In order to make his point, Marcion had to reject the Old Testament and discard much of the New Testament too—all of the gospels, for example, except some of Luke. Jesus, you see, often indicated that the God of the Old Testament was the one he called his Father.

Marcion was excommunicated in about A.D. 144. The church affirmed that the whole Bible is still in effect for us today—the Old Testament as well as the New Testament, which tells us that Jesus Christ and his Father are one (John 10:30). God is just as jealous of his honor and his holiness now as he ever was.

I wonder how much our lives would change if we learned to address God today by the name he revealed to Moses—perhaps not every day, but often enough to keep in the front of our minds the sobering fact that God will not tolerate our worship of anything but himself.

Perhaps if we remembered his jealousy more often, we would notice the depths of our sin more often. And if we remembered his jealousy more often, we would also see more clearly the wonder of the salvation he has provided in Jesus, who came to make it possible for forgetful people like us to be forgiven.

O God whose name is Jealous, how often we transfer to other things the trust and the praise that you alone should receive! Forgive our stubbornness and our blindness. Help us to remember your name Jealous often, and help us to remember there is only one name by which we can be saved—the name of Jesus. Amen.

"Oh, to Be Like Thee!"

"I have set you an example. . . ."
John 13:15

The narrow stairway that leads to the upper room in Jerusalem is nondescript. So is the room itself. When I saw it some years ago, I was not impressed, especially when I remembered that the room the guide showed tourists most likely wasn't the actual room. Even so, the room in which Jesus met with his disciples when he washed their feet was probably much like the one I saw that hot Holy City afternoon.

Whatever that room looked like on the night Jesus and his disciples celebrated the Passover there just hours before his betrayal, there must have been a palpable tension within it. Aside from telling us that a pitcher of water was standing there, John provides scant details about its physical furnishings. They were of no account compared to the spiritual realities that clashed there that night.

There must have been a virtual electricity in the air. Some people, as you may have noticed, have an aura about them. Although they say little or nothing, they convey a message by their demeanor and by a mysterious force that seems to emanate from their person. Besides our ordinary senses, we have a mysterious sense that enables us to feel the reality of another person's attitude, thoughts, and preoccupations.

Examining the room closely, we can tell—ah, yes—that Satan was there. He had entered into Judas's heart—the betrayer's deed was as good as done; there was no turning back. And Christ was there at the peak of his own understanding of who he was and what he had come for. He knew that his Father had put all things under his power and that he had come from God and was returning to him. Eleven other disciples were there as well, vaguely sensing that events were careening toward a horrifying climax—possibly all of Jesus' talk about a cross would soon be actualized. Even so, they were still cruelly selfish.

Seen in the light of the entire Bible, what came together in that room was the eternal God, the Creator of all things, and all the powers of the demonic arrayed against him. Surely everyone there must have sensed that something special was going on. How could it have been otherwise?

That's why it's so striking that just then Jesus—knowing that all things were being delivered into his hands and that he had come from God and was going to him—rose from the table, removed his outer clothing, tied a towel around himself, and (of all things) took the role of a menial servant and washed his disciples' feet. Even Judas's!

How poor these paragraphs are! No words can capture the unique mixture of the grotesque and the sublime expressed within that room. Here was divinity and the satanic rubbing shoulders. Here was the fuse that began to sputter and not cease until the cross was planted and the foot-washer was nailed to its wood. In Jesus' mind was the sickening knowledge that it would take infinite suffering to achieve his victory.

We must not allow our gaze to wander. See what Jesus does. Almighty God becomes a lowly servant. And then . . . when he has finished with the towel and the pitcher (after his embarrassing conversation with Peter), Jesus makes his announcement so that there is no missing the point of what has happened. In effect, he says, "I have set you an example; I expect you to do the same for each other. Now that you know this, you will be blessed if you do it."

It is a holy thing to pray, to sing a psalm, and to read the Bible. It is also a holy thing to be a servant.

Jesus is telling us here that we are like God when we are servants. Those who read the Bible much know that the point is made repeatedly: God became a servant to save his damned people. He rescued them not with a display of his glory but with a display of his humiliation.

Christ is our example. That's the point he made in that supercharged upper room where time, eternity, heaven, and hell came together.

"Oh, to be like thee, blessed Redeemer. . . ."

O Christ Jesus, we cringe as we compare ourselves to you. We don't really want to be servants; we want to be served. Open our eyes to what happened in the upper room. Rescue us from the selfishness that makes us look like Judas. Make us willing to wrap the towel around our waists and to serve others—at home and at work—wherever we are. Please, Lord Jesus. Amen.

$\mathcal{M}$ & $\mathcal{M}$

"Here I am." Exodus 3:4

"I am the Lord's servant." Luke 1:38

The Bible is a people book. It's about God and people. There is just one God, but there are billions of people, and about twenty-five hundred of them are found on the Bible's pages. Among them, M & M are exceptionally fascinating.

Moses and Mary—we should think about them together because they are similar. How can that be? Two people could hardly be more different from each other. Look at these two: Moses, an 80-year-old exiled prince turned shepherd, with his weatherbeaten face; Mary, a winsome young woman, having virtually no experience to mature and mellow her, with face smooth and unlined.

But God made them like brother and sister by startling them when his angel called their names: "Moses, Moses," he said. "Fear not, Mary," he said. And they are alike in their response: "Here I am," said Moses. "Here I am," said Mary—that's what she meant when she said, "I am the Lord's servant."

Different as they are, our brother Moses and sister Mary both stood on the threshold of a great new work of God, and both were used mightily in God's new work. In both cases, it was a work of revelation and salvation.

Romano Guardini, in his book *The Art of Prayer,* classifies Moses' response to God at the burning bush as a prayer. He calls it a prayer of collection. And what is that? A prayer of collection is the response of faith to a sense of the overwhelming manifestation of God's glorious presence. It simply involves placing oneself at God's disposal. It's sort of like running your hands along your sides from your knees up to your chest and then flinging them outward and upward and declaring to the glorious God, "Here I am, O God. I belong to you, body and soul. Do whatever you want with me."

We sometimes speak of "collecting our thoughts." We must also collect ourselves—all of ourselves—and offer ourselves to God each day. Moses and Mary did that. So different from each other as human beings—and yet so very alike. And we, like them, must say, "Here I am, O God. I am your servant. Use me however you will in this new day."

If you know the stories of M & M, you know that their surrenders to God were not without their moments of misgiving and questioning. And as they were involved in God's work of revelation and salvation, both of them stumbled occasionally. Both of them were strong-willed and keen-minded; they could see to the heart of a problem in an instant. And they had their faults, their sins—in Moses' case, his sins kept him out of the land of promise. But both displayed the way God involves his people in his great work of grace. God uses people to accomplish what his grace proposes. His grace qualifies and directs every person he selects for a special mission. Many such people are portrayed on the pages of the Scriptures, and many of them have an importance that transcends the ordinary.

The law came to God's people by Moses; grace and truth came by Mary's Son. Moses became the great mediator who pleaded with God not to destroy his people because of their sin; Mary's Son became the ultimate Mediator, who gave his life to establish the certainty of our salvation.

And it all grew out of a prayer response to God's confrontation. When Moses said, "Here I am," everything changed for him. From that moment on, he was taken up into God's dramatic rescue of his slave people. For Mary too, nothing remained the same after she spoke her obedient response to God. The church through the centuries has called her *theotokos*—"mother of God"—for the child she bore was truly God as well as truly human.

Each day anew, pious men and women follow the example of this faith-filled brother and sister and place themselves before Almighty God in the spirit of surrender. "Here I am," we say. "I am your servant," we say. And the God who has known our names forever will entrust a holy work to us as he did to them, in the light of a burning bush and the glow of an angel's face. And whatever we do in Christ's holy service is his gift to us, not ours to him.

El Shaddai, Jehovah God, we marvel at the way you use people who have been born under the curse. We now present ourselves to you anew this day. Overcome our hesitations and our doubts and be pleased to use us in your holy work. Lord Jesus, Son of God, "be merciful to me, a sinner!" I give myself to your service. In your name, Amen.

Meditation 6

After the Cookies

I desire to . . . be with Christ, which is better by far.

Philippians 1:23

When John watched a video of his 90th birthday, he said to his daughter, "I was pretty good then yet. My voice was pretty good." Now, at 97, there wasn't much left of his voice anymore.

Before his daughter and her husband left, he implored them again to pray every day that God would take him. Sometimes he would ask them to pray right then that he would die and be with Christ at once. "Right now!" he would say, vehement for a few seconds.

One time when he asked them that, he added, "But first I want to eat my cookies. Right after the cookies—let God take me."

He was serious. This old saint knew what he was talking about. For him, Jesus and his Bible were precious as diamonds. He believed the promises: the glory on the other side, the new heaven and the new earth and a new body that would let him talk again without that embarrassing quaver in his voice. He would be able to run and jump—who knows, maybe even fly! He couldn't wait. But he had to. And while he waited, there were the cookies, delicious and fresh, that his daughter brought each time she came; he didn't want to die before he ate those cookies on his plate.

When his daughter told me that he wanted to die after he ate his cookies, we both agreed that perhaps her cookies might hasten his departure since cookies do not have a reputation for extending life. And we agreed that, yes, this is the way it is with those who know the blessed faith. We are somewhat torn. Even the valiant apostle Paul, writing to Philippian Christians from a prison cell, was torn. For him it wasn't cookies but the high call of apostolic duty and the clear call of heaven that brought him turmoil. But if he had lived to 97, even he might have felt a little tug to stay here at least until he had finished his final little pleasure.

So it is with believers: there's the strange intertwining of believing, as Paul did, that it is infinitely better on the other side, while at the same time actually knowing through personal experience only what is on this side—where there is a job to do, where there is a mission to accomplish, where there are loving family and good friends. So we tend to feel that, yes, we are ready to go—in fact, we even want to go—but we would like to hold our little grandchild in our arms or see our daughter's son graduate from high school first . . . or whatever it is that holds us.

To those of us who, like John the cookie lover, are ready to go but would also like to stay at least a little while, the Bible makes a simple statement that we must think about every day: *It is better to be with Christ than to be here.* The important word is *better.* That's because just two things are being compared—here and there. If three things were being compared, we would use the word *best.* But better is correct here because the Bible is talking about what we experience each day and what we will experience when we are with Christ.

Good friend, however attractive it is here, it's better there. It's better for an infinite number of reasons and an eternity of pleasure in God's presence. For those who are sick and dying long before their time, let them know there is no comparison between what we experience here and what God has prepared for those who love him. And for those who are older and still quite strong, who are enjoying life to the full and don't quite want to leave it, let them hear this word of God today: *Being with Christ is better than anything in this world.*

If you are feeling the approach of the final hour, it's wonderfully encouraging that even the apostle Paul felt the tug of this world as he longed for the next. And this man, who had been lifted into glory (2 Cor. 12:1-6), assures us, "It's better over there. Trust me. I know. I've been there." And when you get there, the greatest experiences you ever had in this world will look like cookies in comparison.

Lord of glory, we have our days when we long to begin to experience the everlasting joy you have in store for your people. Thank you for giving us so many dear ones, so much joy here that we often would like to stay longer. Send your Holy Spirit so that we may know with unwavering certainty that it is far better to be with you, loving Savior. In your name, Amen.

Meditation 7

Understanding the Loaves

They had not understood about the loaves.
Mark 6:52

Jesus' disciples were giddy with excitement, relief, and wonder when Jesus, holding Peter upright by the scruff of his neck, clambered over the boat's gunwale in the middle of the lake, and the roar of the wind and the waves stilled instantly, like the way the music stops when a child hits the wrong button on a CD player.

The disciples could hardly process what was happening. A few hours earlier Jesus had commanded them to leave the place where thousands of people had been fed from a food stock of just five loaves and two fish; now they were in big-time trouble as Galilee kicked up a fierce storm. Five- and even eight-foot waves crashed over their small fishing vessel. The gale mocked them as they strained on the oars. They didn't think they were going to make it.

While all this was going on, Jesus was up on a mountainside watching them closely with his divine human eyes that could pierce the dark and the foam and mist that swirled around his disciples. Then he walked through the mountains of waves to help them.

When the disciples saw him, they thought he was a ghost. But when he told them who he was, Peter went overboard to meet the Master, buoyed up by a curious mixture of short-lived faith and bravado that vanished when he heard the laughter of the towering waves. Down he went. He would have been a goner if Jesus hadn't rescued him.

As we read this record, we empathize with the disciples' terror, their confusion, and their vast relief when the wind-ripped fresh water of Galilee became placid. We can understand their reactions perfectly, especially some of us who have despaired at sea or in the air or on a battlefield. But, strangely, the Bible presents all this to show us how dreadfully mistaken the disciples were. There was no excuse for their fear, none whatsoever.

If they had "understood about the loaves," they would have known they could go through any storm as safely as a baby in a crib. But they had a serious problem, these disciples. Their hearts were hardened. Only hours earlier, they had witnessed a miracle of such astonishing proportions that they should never again have doubted that Jesus would take care of them. Remember, he had fed more than five thousand people right before their eyes. After it was all over, there were twelve baskets full of broken pieces of bread and fish—more than they had started with.

Jesus takes care of us. He does. Let there be no doubt about that. And the disciples should have known better. When the wind stiffened and the waves started to kick up, they should have looked at each other and grinned and said, "He'll get us through this . . . he'll get us home."

How many miracles does it take before we disciples of Jesus begin to understand that he surely will take care of us? When we read Mark 6, we learn that Jesus had his eye on his friends every moment. Before he decided it was time to take a walk across Galilee to help them, he saw them.

His eye never leaves us. He wants us to remember not so much his calming of the sea but the loaves. Just remember the loaves. So much of the Christian faith centers on loaves of bread. "Teach us to pray, Jesus," we say, and he answers, "Pray this way: 'Give us this day the bread we need.'" At the last supper he gave us a sacrament of bread and wine as a symbol of his body and blood. And after his resurrection Jesus' disciples suddenly recognized him when he broke bread with them. Then, too, one day while they were eating together, he told them to wait in Jerusalem for the Holy Spirit. And when the Holy Spirit came, the church broke bread together.

When Peter sank beneath the waves, Jesus didn't sympathize. He asked, "Where is your faith?" And Mark's gospel implies that as the supernatural calm settled on their boat, Jesus said something like this: "How come you forgot so quickly? Couldn't you remember what I did just before you cast off? Never forget the loaves. Never. And understand that they mean that I will surely take care of you, no matter what."

Lord Jesus, help us to sense your eye upon us as we journey. When danger looms and we by nature become terrified, help us to remember the loaves. May we not doubt your power and your love for an instant. Every time we take a loaf of bread in our hands, let it be your testimony to us that you will rescue and bring us home safely. Thank you, Jesus. Amen.

Walking Toward Dawn

The path of the righteous is like the first gleam of dawn.

Proverbs 4:18

Blessed are those travelers who often see the birth of day. They begin their journey while stars still shimmer against the pitch of night. The predawn shroud taunts their eyes. But as they journey on, a gentle gray gradually crowds the receding darkness, and soon the new day is upon them.

The first movement in the direction of daylight is hardly noticeable. First the dark shapes of houses and trees become visible. Then street signs take shape, though their messages remain unreadable. Then comes that moment of virtual light just before the first rays of dawn break through and spill across the landscape.

Many years ago Dietrich Bonhoeffer brought Proverbs 4:18 to my attention in his poignant *Letters from Prison*. It's not a statement confirmed by experience in the cold and dark of prison, where Bonhoeffer was shut up for speaking the message of righteousness. In such a place "the path of the righteous" would hardly seem to be "like the first gleam of dawn" that shines brighter as it moves toward the light of day. God's people take note of this statement simply because God has declared it to be true and has made sure it's included in the canon.

The reality of darkness giving way to the splendor of sunrise is not connected to how pleasant and comfortable our situation happens to be at any given time. Our night-talk and our dawn-talk is about vision. It's about what we see, not about how pleasant or unpleasant life can be. And people of faith have unique vision. While life can have its terrifying side at any given moment, believers see the light of life not because of their experience but because of God and the faith God has given them.

As believers move along their various paths, they do not in fact experience less trial—they experience more. As their exposure to illness and accident and family sorrow increases with each passing year, they are often dreadfully uncomfortable. Their sometimes wretched circumstances can wrap their souls in darkest night. Yet faith in Christ can make each block of time bring growing certainty that God will surely overspread their life with light.

The vision of approaching dawn is planted in the hearts of those for whom Christ is the ultimate reality. Admittedly, whenever we declare that we are moving toward the dawn, we can never be sure there are no calamities lurking in the darkness that will render our statement foolish. When I think about this statement, as I have done countless times over the years, I have no way of knowing what suffering could be my lot. I know the suffering I have experienced, and I can still say the words of Proverbs 4:18, but I know not what future misery there could be. We make faith statements, however, when we are absolutely certain of something we cannot see. God is the one who says I am moving toward dawn's beauty, and I believe him.

Yes, faith statements often seem contradicted by reality. When Bonhoeffer referred to Proverbs 4:18, he did not know he would be executed just one day before the carnage of World War II would cease. What irony!

And I think of Charlie, who lives in a home for the elderly, sitting outside in the winter cold on his folding chair, taking deep drags on the cigarettes that still enslave him, and telling me, when I greet him, that he would love to die and go to Jesus. There is little of dawn's bright light on Charlie's wrinkled face.

There's a humbling mystery in the miseries of life that is not easily solved. Yet, as the dawn of our eternal day is about to break upon us, the darkness begins to give way to the predawn gray, and we begin to see what we never saw before. There begins to grow within our heart of hearts the surety that the pain and suffering will pass. And there are unmistakable evidences that what has been promised us will surely happen. We believe that what we now experience is just the first part of a journey that will forever be bathed in splendor.

As we continue to make our way through this dark night, O Son of God, please show us, however faintly, the beginnings of the dawn of the eternal day. Help us see intimations of the glorious future before us. O risen and glorified Savior, we know it has been your pain and sorrow that make the wondrous dawn so certain. In your name, Amen.

Meditation 9

Stolyarov

"Men loved darkness instead of light. . . ."
John 3:19

Our memories of some sentences or passages in the Bible are often associated with a person or situation that has drawn our attention to them. We cannot read those sentences in Scripture without remembering that person or situation. That's the way it is for me with this solemn sentence: "This is the verdict: Light has come into the world, but men loved darkness instead of light because their deeds were evil." I shall always associate this with Major General Nikolai Stolyarov of the Russian Air Force.

Several of us were sitting in my living room discussing some of the details of a speaking tour the general was taking through the midwestern United States. We were conversing in English, and he was sitting on the sofa in my living room reading a Russian New Testament. Suddenly his hand shot out, and he interrupted us. "Ah-hah!" he exclaimed. "This is it. This is the truth: 'Light has come into the world, but men loved darkness instead of light.'"

He spoke in rapid Russian; Alex Leonovich translated his intense words for us. I was stunned. Could this be happening . . . in my own living room? It was astonishing that General Stolyarov was there, it was even more astonishing that he was reading the Bible, and it was more astonishing still that he of all people would pounce on John 3:19 and announce that it is the truth.

I had first met him less than a year earlier in Moscow when a group of us evangelical Christians were ushered into the KGB's large briefing room above the Lubianka prison. Stolyarov was then the deputy director of the KGB, and when he strode into the room, we were impressed by the aura that surrounded him and his military bearing. President Gorbachev had elevated him to the rank of major general and had given him this high ranking job with the KGB because Stolyarov had remained faithful to him during the ill-fated coup of August 1991; in fact, Stolyarov, we were told, had piloted the airplane that had brought Gorbachev back from the Crimea after the coup fizzled.

That evening there had been prayer in the KGB headquarters, and when I had talked with Stolyarov, I had invited him to come to Chicago and appear on the "Faith 20" telecast of the Back to God Hour. At the time, I never thought he would accept the invitation. But it all worked out, and so it was that we traveled through the midwestern U.S., where he addressed college students and others about the future of the new Russia, a future that we now know was never to occur.

I cannot vouch for Stolyarov's faith, but of his high interest in the Bible and the Christian faith there can be no doubt. God used him to arrange to have the Bible published in a special edition for Russian soldiers. And this man knew, better than anyone in my living room that November afternoon, that humankind has surely rejected the light and has loved darkness instead.

Just what is happening in Russia today is hard to say. It seems that its brief foray into the light is coming to an end and that treacherous forces are again on the rise. During this century that nation has been severely tortured, and the torture it has endured has come from an evil and fierce ideology that has corrupted its people and its institutions for centuries. The perverting power of totalitarianism has rendered this great people incapable of building a new nation in which the light of the gospel illumines the landscape.

But enough of Russia. We must look at our own nations in North America. Our nations too have their love affair with darkness. The marvelous technology and high standard of living we enjoy have not built nations in which the glorious truth of Jesus is embraced by all. By no means. In place of the brilliance of divine truth, which is there for all who wish to seek it, we have become a continent held in the embrace of an evil materialism.

So "the verdict" is true—not because Stolyarov endorsed it—but because the Bible is always right. We are lovers of that which threatens us with eternal death. The light has come—Jesus, God's own Son—but we are enamored of trivialities. The darkness is becoming impenetrable. Only those who walk with Jesus, the light of the world, have reason to hope.

Lord, look upon General Stolyarov in this day and give him your salvation. Hear this prayer also for his nation, which seems to be stumbling toward disaster again. And look at us on this continent, who so often love what is unworthy. Help us to love Jesus, the light of the world. We pray in his name, Amen.

Christ of the Nations

"Nations will come to your light. . . ."
Isaiah 60:3

Old Testament prophecy is one of the most exciting proofs that Jesus Christ of Nazareth is the Son of the living God. The virgin-born son of the adoptive father Joseph did not come unexpectedly; centuries of prophetic utterance, at least one of them going all the way back to Eden, told of Christ's coming.

Isaiah was a prime example of someone who told of Christ's coming. Already in the seventh chapter of his book of prophecy, the virgin birth is foretold. And later, in chapter 9, we learn that the Messiah would bring the light of God to nations living in darkness and that there would be several wondrous names by which he would be called. Still later, in chapter 53, we see the horrifying specter of the Christ's wrath-death. And in chapter 60, we read about a light coming upon the nations that could be no one but our Savior. Chapter 61 begins with words Jesus took upon his own lips, and, after reading them, he declared that he fulfilled that prophecy.

But the telling forth of God's truth was not only expressed by mainline Jewish prophets; others of non-Jewish background also spoke the word of the Lord. Some of their prophecies are found in the Bible. Jethro, Moses' father-in-law, a Midianite, was captured by Moses' faith; so was Ruth the Moabite maid. Balaam, a non-Jewish prophet who was, sad to say, more in love with money than he was with God, talked about Israel's glorious future, even though he really didn't want to.

And within the early church there were those who thought they found among earlier, unbelieving poets certain intimations that Christ was coming. Augustine, for example, thought this way about the Roman poet Virgil, who lived from 70-19 B.C. Virgil wrote about a virgin-born child whose birth would change the world. Historian Jaroslav Pelikan tells how Virgil spoke of the arrival of a "new order of the ages," which would occur through the birth of a child from a virgin. Because of this child's work, Virgil said, there would be "a new human race . . . descending from the heights of heaven." Virgil believed that this child would bring about the transformation of humankind. Note what he wrote: "Under your guidance, whatever vestiges remain of our ancient wickedness,/ Once done away with, shall free the earth from its incessant fear." Continuing, the poet said, "For your sake, O child, the earth, without being tilled/ Will freely pour forth its gifts." Virgil called this child the "child of the gods." Remarkable, isn't it, that this unbeliever would have had a vision of a child who would come to right all wrongs, born of a virgin? Augustine was confident that this was already a prophecy about the coming of Christ.

Scholars deal with these facts today in various ways, but there is enough here to see that somewhere within the soul of the human race there's a longing for a Savior who will look exactly like Jesus Christ. As the church proclaimed Christ to the nations, it assumed that the rest of the world was waiting for him. The church knew the world needed him.

Our Lord Jesus is the answer to the deepest questions humankind has always asked. If nothing else, Virgil's poetry confirms that all the human race, even those outside of Israel, were asking for events that only the Messiah could accomplish. And still today, as we bring the message of the Savior to the ends of the earth, we may believe that no person, no tribe, no nation is so different from all other human beings that the gospel of Jesus Christ will not be the word of life to them.

The Christ we love and serve is the Christ for the nations. He was the Christ the very moment he was born. Even then not only the Jews but also the entire world was waiting for him. And people are waiting for him still today. Jesus comes with light—not just for people like us but for all the nations of the world.

O Lord, we are thrilled to learn that before you were born, even unbelievers were longing for a child like you. Make us excited, O Christ, about your worldwide power and your desire to draw all people to yourself. May those of us who know you share the message of your love eagerly with those who live near us. And may we never falter as we seek to bring your message of life to the entire world. In your name, Amen.

Holy Bread

They devoted themselves . . . to the breaking of bread. . . .

Acts 2:42

Before the family began to eat their salad and spaghetti, the big burly father turned to the preacher and asked, "Would you grace the meal for us?" So the preacher "graced" the meal with a prayer, and then everyone joined in. Even the baby seemed to enjoy what was going on.

Some people view saying grace before a meal as a superstition you outgrow when you get older. When we think about it, though, it's a holy moment that more than likely goes back to what people did at the very beginning of this era when they were filled with the Holy Spirit. They became devoted people whose lives were focused on several important events, and one of them was "the breaking of bread."

Bible scholars will tell you that this item among the four in Acts 2:42 refers to the celebration of the Lord's Supper, the Eucharist. And that is likely true. But that is probably not the whole story.

The whole story more than likely has something to do with the way Jesus, who had just left them and sent them his Holy Spirit, had made eating together a high point in their lives. Those who know the Bible well can tick off special occasions with Christ that centered on a meal: the wedding at Cana, the feeding of the five thousand, the feeding of the four thousand, the meal at a Pharisee's house, lots of meals at the home of Mary and Martha, the Last Supper, Jesus' breaking bread and eating fish with his disciples on Resurrection evening, a breakfast of bread and fish at the Sea of Galilee when Jesus reinstated Peter as an apostle, the meal at which Jesus promised the coming of the Holy Spirit. There are other occasions too, and when you look at them, you see that just having a meal must have brought back many rich memories to the men and women who had been close to Jesus during his earthly ministry. It wouldn't be surprising, then, if those people in the early church, whose lives were transformed totally by Christ's

Holy Spirit, thought of Jesus whenever they had their meals. They surely couldn't "break bread," as they called it, without remembering the times Jesus did it. Some of them remembered the startling revelation of his glorified divinity that burst on them when he ate with them: "When he was at the table with them, he took bread, gave thanks, broke it and began to give it to them. Then their eyes were opened and they recognized him . . ." (Luke 24:30-31).

Faith in Jesus transforms the ordinary moments of life into holy moments, ordinary bread into holy bread. Sitting in the Burger King built over I-294 outside Chicago, you can watch people plunk themselves down and start eating their fries before they get their chair they way they want it beneath the table, attacking their burger as if they're refueling like the Peterbilts that rumble by beneath their feet. But children of Pentecost can pause even there to remember their Savior, who ate so often with his children, and they can invite him to join them in that humble place: "Holy Jesus, be our guest. . . ." So they grace their food before they eat it.

The sacramental meal we call the Lord's Supper is an unusually significant time of eating—one so powerfully strong that we call it a "means of grace." But an ordinary meal can be powerfully strong in its own way when it is graced by Jesus' presence. And surely there is reason to pray when we eat these days, with the growing confusion about just what is healthful and what is not—there's good reason to ask the Lord to bless our food and drink.

One thing is certain: one of the results of the Holy Spirit's coming was that the simple act of breaking bread took on new meaning. We might expect that an event so pivotal and life-changing as Pentecost would have left Christ's followers starry-eyed, hardly in touch with reality. But no—it left them thinking of Jesus with special intensity when they ate their ordinary food. They remembered. And I am sure they paused to thank him and ask him to join them yet again and fill their meal with grace.

Lord Jesus, thank you for coming to this humdrum world of ours and sitting down again and again with your people. As we eat our humble food once more, direct our thoughts to those precious moments when you broke bread with your followers and, while doing so, taught them many things and showed them the splendor of your divinity. Grace our days and every meal, we pray. Amen.

Convicted

"You are the man!"
2 Samuel 12:7

The two chapters in the Bible that make me cringe the most are Genesis 3, which describes humankind's fall into sin, and 2 Samuel 11, which describes King David's sin of coveting, adultery, lying, and murder. His lust for Bathsheba, his adultery with her, and his despicable murder of her husband represent the depths of human depravity. The fact that a man so highly favored by God would commit such gross sin defies explanation. That he did it and that he hid it from others and himself baffles us.

If you wish to preserve a laundered and romanticized picture of David, 1 and 2 Samuel should be off-limits for you. You might as well stay away from 1 Chronicles too. But a sanitized David will not help us much. When we examine the behavior of the real David, we discover the results of Genesis 3—the fearsome results of the fall into sin are there for everyone to see in David's life and in the lives of his family members who also committed murder and adultery.

So it was that God sent Nathan to confront David with his sin, and the king's repentance and remorse have become a pattern for fallen sinners to follow. Psalms 32 and 51 are generally viewed as David's laments about how far he had fallen. Christians today, convicted of their sin, embrace these psalms and use their fervent plea for mercy: "Have mercy on me, O God . . . . I know my transgressions, and my sin is always before me. . . . Cleanse me . . ." (Ps. 51:1-7).

Jesus is called "the Son of David" in the Bible, and that means he not only established David's kingdom forever but also paid for all of David's sin, including his behavior described in 2 Samuel 11.

Yes, David's Son, the Messiah, Jesus Christ, died for David's sin and for the sins of all who believe in him. And the sordid record of David's plunge into the depths of depravity is there for us to examine so that, when we do, we will receive a strange comfort. David's stubborn resolve to go on as if nothing were wrong after he had murdered and committed adultery is a reminder of how profoundly sick we can become. An examination of David's degenerate acts encourages us to look closely at our own lives and to confess the most disgusting of our own sins. We are summoned to go beyond the ordinary meanness and anger that we usually allow ourselves to think of when we think of our sin. And no matter how evil we have become, we can confess and receive divine forgiveness.

The simple hymn that assures conscience-stricken failures with the words "There is room at the cross for you" is telling the truth. There is room. And there is room there for all who confess their sins, no matter how grievous those sins may be, because Jesus Christ, David's Son, came to change everything. Not only did he come to make forgiveness possible, but he also came to make it possible for believers to live more faithfully than David did.

We must not forget that although David was a child of God and he had received God's Spirit so that he could be Israel's king, the simplest believer today has the Holy Spirit more constantly and intensely than David did. This side of Pentecost, the Holy Spirit comes to live within us; he makes us his temple.

The apostle John says, "We know that anyone born of God does not continue to sin; the one who was born of God keeps him safe, and the evil one cannot harm him. We know that we are children of God, and that the whole world is under the control of the evil one. We know also that the Son of God has come and has given us understanding, so that we may know him who is true. And we are in him who is true—even in his Son Jesus Christ" (1 John 5:18-20). David was as he was because the Holy Spirit had not yet been poured out fully. Christ lived, died, rose again, and ascended into heaven so that those who believe in him today can live ever more faithfully and gloriously.

Forgive us, we pray, O God of all mercy. We are thinking of our ordinary sins, and we also see a reflection of ourselves in David's sin and blindness. Help us to be candid with you and with ourselves, O God. And help us to receive the ministry of your Holy Spirit within us so that we may be kept from falling as David did. We pray in Christ's name, Amen.

Take Off Your Clothes

"Take off his filthy clothes."
Zechariah 3:4

We really do need preachers, preachers who bring us the Word of God in all its fullness and power.

I realized that again when I heard my friend Jacob Eppinga preach on Zechariah 3. When a preacher brings the gospel in its power and fullness, it's almost as if you'd died and gone to heaven.

In his inimitable way, Eppinga related Zechariah 3 to a story that Leo Tolstoy told in one of his great novels. I won't relate the story completely, but at one point in it a king, who wanted to know more about God, asked a peasant, who had already told him much about God, "What does God do?" And the peasant told the king, "I cannot tell you what God does, unless we exchange our clothes." The king, though puzzled, had reason to trust the peasant, and he proceeded to put his crown on the peasant's head and put the peasant's cap on his own head. The king did the same with his beautiful robe—he took the peasant's, and the peasant took his. And so on. And then the peasant said: "This is what God does. God takes our unworthy garments upon himself and clothes us in his own splendor."

Tolstoy's simple story, when tied with the sentences that open Zechariah 3, makes you catch your breath as you suddenly understand that yes, indeed, this is exactly what this passage is all about. It's exactly what the cross of Calvary is all about.

As Joshua stands before the blazing holiness of God, with Satan right there announcing Joshua's unworthiness to be near God, God arranges for Joshua's filthy clothes to be exchanged for clothes that are stunningly brilliant with divine righteousness.

If you read the first six verses of Zechariah 3, please understand that the "angel of the Lord" figure is an appearance of God himself. And in the angel's words, "See, I have taken away your sin, and I will put rich garments on you," we hear the word of God Almighty, our merciful Father in heaven.

The exchange of the filthy garments of sin for the rich garments of salvation vividly portrays what happened when God came to this earth in the Son of his love, Jesus Christ. See him hanging on the cross. He is naked, but not naked—he is clothed with all the filthy garments of all us filthy people who have sinned against God so often that we have lost count. We often have sinned against God so stupidly that we haven't even known we were doing so when we sinned. God takes our filthy garments and gives us his own royal robes to wear in their place.

All this is a marvel beyond reckoning. And there's something especially overwhelming when this message obliterates your pride as you sit among the faithful and you hear a preacher bring the Word of grace. Sermons must bring together the holy ingredients of sacred Scripture so that they strike us with an intensity we cannot experience any other way.

Jesus said that whenever two or three are gathered in his name, he will be there. A worship service is a special time when God's people gather, each one knowing in at least some degree that he or she has a need that can be filled only through the ministry of the Bible. So the people sing, and they pray for the presence of the Savior, and the preacher prays that God will use his study and preparation in the minutes set aside for the preaching of the Word. And the Bible is opened. And the preacher speaks. And suddenly, almost like an explosion deep within you, the message captures you again.

What does God do? He tells me to take off my clothes, which stink with the filth of sin, and he gives me the royal robes of righteousness to wear instead. The cross has made this blessed exchange possible and real.

Lord God who spoke to Joshua in Zechariah's vision, please supply us with preachers who have been so captivated by the message of salvation through the cross that they tell us about it again and again. Humble our high and mighty hearts and help us see how filthy are the garments we wear by nature and how desperately we need Christ's royal robe. In his name, Amen.

Hope Without Disappointment

Hope does not disappoint us. . . .
Romans 5:5

There are several emotional states that go by the name *hope* that are not hope. Hope in its pure form is uplifting and buoyant. Experiencing it is like drinking deeply of a delicious, cool nectar when you are desperately thirsty. You exhale and murmur, "Aah . . . this is wonderful!"

When the apostle Paul speaks about hope that does not disappoint us, he does so after describing the blessing nobody wants: suffering. We tend to arrange our lives so that we insure as much as possible that we will escape suffering. We watch our diets, we sometimes even exercise, and we meticulously monitor our finances to make sure we live as comfortably as we can. Many people manage to avoid affliction most of their lives. Can't blame them for that. But here's a secret: so long as you feel comfortable and secure, whatever you call hope isn't hope in its pure form.

It's startling to find the apostle's discussion of suffering in Romans 5 because he has been talking about another subject all along. The big subject here is *justification by faith;* then suddenly he veers in the direction of pain and misery. In the end it seems that he is setting up an equation here that looks something like this: Those who are justified by faith have peace with God, and this makes it possible for them, even when they go through suffering, to experience hope. And the hope he's talking about is the sweet smell of heaven that you can have while you are in this world.

Let's be frank about this: it is impossible to experience this hope so long as events are going smoothly. To be sure, you can know about the glory God has for his people, and you can even believe you are going to experience it someday, but when everything is going well, all of this glory talk remains in the realm of the theoretical. As long as hope is in that realm, you cannot taste its sweetness and feel it run through your whole self, body and soul, like the energy of God.

As long as we depend on our usual supports, the fullness of hope eludes us. Young people depend on the strength of their youth to get them through. Middle-aged people depend on their pharmacist to supply the "little helpers" they need to get them through. Older people expect that modern medicine will step in with just what they need when they get their heart attack or cancer. As long as these supports are there, they impede our experience of the hope that does not disappoint.

Because suffering gradually (and sometimes not so gradually) strips away everything that props up our lives, it finally leaves us with hope alone. When we come to the place where everything else has proved incapable of helping us further, we can fall back into the arms of God and say, "Oh yes, now I know what you have meant all along. I can depend on you. I can trust you. I know, I know you are going to take care of me."

When it occurs within the good providence of God that protects his children, suffering produces perseverance and character and hope. This hope is strong and exciting because it comes from God himself. It does not disappoint because it is caused by the infusion of divine love by the Holy Spirit within our hearts. This hope is supernatural.

It is difficult to be a Christian in this age, not because there are so many temptations to sin against God (though that is a problem) but because there are so many things in this age that promise to take care of us. We read the ads: "Trust me, I will take care of your financial situation until you die." "Trust me, I will get rid of your varicose veins." "Trust me, I will get rid of your insomnia." "Trust me, I will help you get rid of your boredom." "Trust me, I will take care of you." The clamor is incessant. And it all distracts us from the hope that will never disappoint. We must trust God fully, totally, leaning on him only. Suffering can cause rejoicing because it is able to take you to the point where you have to do that.

O loving God, we want to feel the white-hot power of the hope that never disappoints. Do we dare ask you to do whatever is necessary to allow us to experience this? We do not dare. Yet we want to be startled by the over-powering reality of the hope that really is hope. Make the reality of divine love real within us, O Holy Spirit. Amen.

The Road to Mercy City

Build roads to [the cities of refuge].
Deuteronomy 19:3

In the United States, Republicans and Democrats alike have been changed by events that occurred during the reign of a Republican general whose name was Eisenhower. The great legacy of his presidency is the national system of interstate highways. Few developments have had as much impact on the North American continent. If the interstate highways in the U.S. had never been built, the automobile industry would be different, metropolitan areas would be larger, suburbia would be smaller, and even the relationship of people at various income levels would be different. Since the 1950s the nation has been transformed by its roads.

We have a love-hate relationship with this great highway system. It makes it possible for us to travel just about anywhere in the country, but it also aggravates us because of the incessant repair work required and the far too frequent gridlocks that frustrate us. But roads are marvelous creations of humankind, and they are especially marvelous when they are built in order to achieve divine purposes.

As the people of Israel prepared to enter the promised land, God, through Moses, instructed them to make sure they built roads to special cities. Of course they would have their ordinary roads—they would appear between locations to which people traveled regularly. So this is not a command to build roads in general—they would do that in any case. But God wanted to make sure that his special cities of mercy would be accessible.

When one takes the time to read the Pentateuch, the first five books of the Bible, there is something touching about the establishment of six cities of refuge, which were to be given to the Levites and were to be places where a person could flee if he caused someone's death. The very establishment of these cities envisioned an industrious and thriving nation, in which people rose early and sometimes toiled late in order to plant their fields, bring in their harvests, and build their homes. It would be a nation of workers. And sometimes, inadvertently, there would be accidents that would make you gasp; suddenly someone would be dead, with a gash across the chest, or an ugly bruise on the head and a trickle of blood coming from the corner of his mouth.

What to do? The law among the ancient Israelites allowed for an avenger of blood—often the brother of the dead man—to pursue the person who had caused the man's death and to kill him. So God provided safety for those who might kill someone accidentally. There were special cities of mercy to which they could flee; there they would be protected, and after the death of the high priest, they could leave the city and no one would have a right to touch them.

But, of course, there had to be a way to get to those cities. So God commanded, "You must make sure there are roads to the cities of mercy. These are, in a sense, the most important roads you will ever build, O Israel. They are the way along which the fear-filled and wretched killers will flee to safety. And, once there, they will be sheltered by the mercy of the Lord."

Those who fled to cities of refuge in those days to escape the fury of the avengers of blood were innocent. But what of us who are not innocent of the crimes uncovered by heaven's holy light in our lives? We too may flee to the city of mercy. And we must travel the road of God's own grace, pointed out to us in Jesus' words: "I am the way and the truth and the life. No one comes to the Father except through me" (John 14:6).

He who directs us to the mercy-filled road is the heavenly High Priest himself, whose sacrificial death frees those who believe in him from all their guilt and fear. Those who walk the Jesus Road shall surely arrive at the mercy-filled city of God, where they will find relief and joy infinitely more liberating than anything discovered by those who staggered into a city of refuge.

God of all mercy, we are touched by your tenderness as we see your response to our busy lives in which we so often make serious mistakes and commit grievous sins. We praise you now as we remember Christ, your Son, who has become the way, the truth, and the life for us. Receive us now, we pray, as we run to your refuge of forgiveness in Jesus' name. Amen.

Omri

Omri did evil in the eyes of the LORD. . . .
1 Kings 16:25

Nobody names their son Omri, perhaps mainly because we don't know or hear much about Omri. David, yes, and Solomon and Caleb are well-known, and parents still name their boys after these famous Israelites. But Omri is not only buried somewhere in Israel; he's also buried away in the Bible, obscure and discarded. This is strange because Omri was one of the really great kings of Israel. We have to go to sources outside the Bible, though, to find that out.

Omri was really an impressive guy. He accomplished more in the twelve years he was king of Israel than most people do in an entire lifetime. He got rid of his rival, whose name was Tibni, purchased the land for a new capital and constructed most of it, re-conquered lost territory, and entered into important alliances with foreign powers. The Bible pays him scant heed, but while he was doing his thing, he was a mover and a shaker.

We learn about Omri from the Moabite Stone, which tells how he conquered Moab. Scholars report the following about Omri's accomplishments: "Archaeological excavations have uncovered sizable portions of the Israelite capital: strong and intricate fortifications, a sumptuous palace quarter, storehouses and sundry administrative installations. We are left with an impression of might and prosperity." Even 150 years later, important world leaders still called Israel "the house of Omri."

The Bible's dominant impression of this mighty man, however, is found in 1 Kings 16:25, which tells us that Omri did more evil than any king before him. God is not impressed with the building of city capitals, nor with the vanquishing of mighty armies, nor with the international treaties of a world ruler. The writer of 1 Kings, which, according to the *Geneva Study Bible,* was completed midway through the exile a couple of centuries after Omri's illustrious twelve-year reign, most likely knew of Omri's international reputation but chose not to give it the slightest attention. Omri was a rebel against the true God. Every other fact about him was secondary. His faith, his heart, his daily walk were what was important.

Even though we do not name our children after this impressive king nowadays, we live in an age in which we are tempted to become just like him. Achievement is measured the same way now as it was then. Even when we think of God's people in the church today, we tend to let our eyes rest on those within it who have done many Omri-like deeds—built empires, exerted great influence, amassed wealth.

Nothing is more necessary for us than to look at life as the Bible does. What impresses us does not impress God. He looks within our hearts; our attitude is what counts. Do we love him? Do we think about him? Do we earnestly seek to understand his will for us and diligently seek to do his will? Nothing is more important than seeking to live as God wants us to.

As we respond to the Bible's description of Omri and we think of the way God examines our lives, we are jolted back to reality. Anything we have done that we can be proud of, any possessions we have acquired, even if for good, that we have literally grown to love—none of these will survive God's scrutiny if our hearts are evil and wicked.

In many ways the Bible tells us what is truly important: living for God. Thus it contradicts the way the world today looks at human beings and their lives. For God, the great question is whether people like us are seeking his kingdom or seeking their own. Omri, for all his accomplishments and fame, was in the service of the kingdom of Satan. So even though world leaders many decades later still referred to his successes, Omri died a dismal failure.

That's what happens to those who displace God with idols. Though none of us carries the name Omri, the history of this evil and successful man is in the Bible as a warning for us who are a lot more like him than we care to admit.

Almighty God, help us to realize that there is much we can learn from Omri's life and times. Through your Holy Spirit within us, help us to adjust our thinking and our actions so that we seek to do your will above all else. Help us to understand that you disdain what we often exalt. Forgive our sins, O gracious God, and save us this day. For Jesus' sake, Amen.

Sustained by God

Cast your cares on the LORD. . . .

Psalm 55:22

Pain changes people. When you have a plain, ordinary headache, it wrecks your day and you act differently. When people have excruciating back pain, day after day, they are not the same persons they were without it. When you have pain, there's only one thing on your mind: relief. I'll be happy to have a root canal, thank you, if it will relieve my pain. Lead me to the most frightening operation, and I'll go willingly if it will take my pain away.

When you are dealing with horrible pain, you don't care to hear much from people who have never had it. What do they know about it? You try to be polite when they talk to you, but inside you cringe. They will never know what you are going through. They will never know the bliss that comes when the nurse gives you a shot, and finally, finally, the pain ebbs away.

The Bible is full of pain—pain of all kinds. Many of the psalms are anguished cries from people who are being tormented. Psalm 55 stands out as one that is about psychological distress. We associate it with David, and there were times in his life when he screamed to high heaven because of the way events were going against him. The writer of this psalm is distraught, cringing before the terrors of death, shaking with fear and trembling, crying out to God in his distress.

In this regard, then, the writer is everyman, everywoman. Most people go through times like these. And those of us who know the fierce cruelty of physical or mental pain—or both of these—cannot help being somewhat startled by the simple command at the end of the psalm: "Cast your cares on the LORD and he will sustain you." Sufferers wouldn't take this from just anyone; they would have to know that the person speaking to them had been through agony. Well, we know that's true in this case. And the writer here, himself doubled up in misery, says, "Give it all over to the Lord."

"Cast your cares"—the Hebrew word for *cares* here is used only once in the Bible. It refers to cares in the broadest, widest sense—not just the specific item that causes you discomfort right now, but that item and all the other cares you have. When we are distressed by something physical, mental, emotional, or whatever, and that something is affecting everything else in our lives, we are told here to cast our *everything* on the Lord and that he will sustain us.

Will that help? Well, there it is in black and white and inspired by the Holy Spirit: *God will sustain.*

Pain researchers nowadays are making important discoveries on how they can treat the torturous pain some people endure. They check the nerve pathways that lead from the injured area to the spine and up into the brain, and they devise blockers that will thwart the merciless enemy. Psalm 55 is in another realm. The main idea in the psalmist's word "sustain" is total care, with no detail overlooked.

We are to cast our *everything* on God—all our stressors and troubles—and he will respond with what is needed to carry us through. He may take the pain away; he may not. But one thing is certain: he will sustain faith-filled people when they turn their *everything* over to him.

We must understand that these are not just words here, as though they are a suitably spiritual response dreamed up by a poet as something that would make a good ending for a poem dealing with agony. This is the Holy Spirit's word sent our way by the God who suffered more than any of us ever will.

The suffering of Christ was an experience of his entire being, in which his blessed divinity sustained his anguished humanity. It was the divine that enabled him to endure death and hell and brought him through to the glorious freshness of victory.

We who suffer now must turn our everything over to Christ, and he will sustain us as he was sustained. Can we ask for anything more?

Merciful God, we bow before you in our deep need. You know our every pain, whether it be physical, mental, or emotional—and all of these together. Enter our broken lives with your power and enable us to surrender our total selves to you. We ask for relief. We ask for your sustaining presence. Please, O Christ, care for us today. Amen.

Great Is Diana

"Great is Artemis of the Ephesians!"
Acts 19:34

If you read Acts 19:34 in the English translation that came from Princess Diana's native land—that is, the King James Version—you'll find that it reads, "Great is Diana!" Artemis/Diana was the fertility goddess of many breasts, worshiped throughout the Roman empire and enshrined in a stunning temple in Ephesus. Is there a connection between the Princess of Wales and the idol that stood in the Ephesian temple?

One thing is sure—in the attention given the untimely death of Diana Spencer, there is something we must learn about human nature. Never was a monarch or high government official buried with greater honor. The funeral ceremonies in London were echoed in satellite ceremonies throughout the world; the church service there was echoed in Chicago, Toronto, Los Angeles, and elsewhere.

And when it was all over, those who thought deeply about what had happened pointed out with some hesitation and embarrassment that this woman had done nothing to explain the lavish attention she received in death. To say this is not to demean her; it is simply being realistic. It has been said often that "she was famous for being famous." Surely in the world's reaction to her death, we learn more about ourselves than we learn about her.

And what we learn is that humanity still needs a goddess. This unusually attractive and socially gifted woman surely did not deliberately create the extraordinary adulation that arose for her. On a certain level, the cause of her death was very ordinary; she became another victim of the killer alcohol. People who entrust themselves to those who use it live dangerously. So she lived, and so she died.

If we want to explain what it was that caused the universal outpouring of love for her, we must not look at her; we must look elsewhere. As some have pointed out, in some ways the media created her and the media destroyed her. The *paparazzi* exploited her and pursued her to her death. On the day Diana was buried, a distraught nonagenarian called me and bemoaned the fact that no one talked about her as a person, about her soul; they simply assumed she had been translated to heaven. Who could say anything about her eternal destiny? Did she pray? Did she love Jesus? Were there times in her life when she turned to God and asked him for forgiveness? We don't know; no one ever told us that. The media was not interested in that.

In the universal cry "Great is Diana," we find our age taking up the ageslong cry of idol worshipers. And in ancient times it was the female idols that aroused the greatest frenzy. An idol then, of course, was purely the creation of human imagination. Idols do not represent reality; human beings make them with their minds and then worship them. So, in our age, the media conspire to create people who are bigger than life. The creation has virtually nothing to do with who these people actually are. They become imaginary people, and humankind idolizes them.

The grief of the Spencers and the continuing conflict between them and the house of Windsor are surely causes for sadness. Sadder still is the specter of two young men deprived of their mother's influence. And saddest of all is the sudden death of a 36-year-old woman who had been cruelly used, a woman who likely never had a chance to learn who she really was. Now she is gone, a person who awakened pity among us often because of her pathetic life.

Those of us who want more than anything to be formed by the Bible must understand that the great driving power that incited the Ephesians to frenzied rioting still drives the masses to attach their adoration to unworthy images. For an anguished and intense September week in 1997, Diana Spencer became the modern counterpart of the image housed in the temple in Ephesus two thousand years ago.

Idolatry is not dead. It is still a powerful force among us, and those who believe in Christ and the Bible have a lifelong obligation to resist idolatry with all the strength the Holy Spirit gives.

Holy Spirit, come into our lives and make us smart enough to understand what is going on in our world. May we realize that the same realities confronted by the early church are still among us. Spirit of the living God, we ask you to comfort those who sorrow because of Diana's death. And use what happened to help all of us understand ourselves better. In Jesus' name, Amen.

Nasty Families

"There was a man who had two sons. . . ."

Luke 15:11

Is there a parable better known than the parable of the prodigal son? It's the centerpiece of Jesus' parable ministry, it's rich with detail, and each detail invites us to ponder what it stands for. One of the fascinating things this parable does for us is let us look deep into the mind of the person telling the story. Let's look at it today in order to understand that wonderful mind.

Read a short story or a novel, and you will learn something about the author. Charles Dickens wrote *Little Dorritt* when his own marriage was falling apart; the novel has several disintegrating marriages in it. In Jesus' story of the wastrel son, we see into Jesus' mind.

The story, of course, was one of those unique stories designed to reveal the kingdom of God to some and to hide it from others. It is puzzling that Jesus did this—but he did, and we must accept that. The fact that he told stories designed both to hide and reveal must have something to do with God's deepest will, which is unfathomable for us.

What does Jesus reveal of his own interior life in this parable in which he deftly paints the picture of a wealthy man with two sons? In the first part of the parable we learn that the younger son was a scoundrel. He had no parental love or respect. He was a selfish, covetous spendthrift who visited whores.

This foul kid had actually gone to his dad and had brazenly asked him for his share of the inheritance while the father was in full possession of his faculties. What he did was a gross violation of at least four of the Ten Commandments, to say nothing of its being so cold and unfeeling that it makes your skin crawl just to think of it.

This insolent son existed in Jesus' mind. He drew this character. And what this tells us is that Jesus perfectly knew us and how we act and what we go through. The details of this parable indicate that the Son of God was thoroughly a part of the society he had been born into, and his precise picture of the younger son shows that he knew our human nature.

The simple truth is that children often treat their parents outrageously. They did so when Jesus was here, and they do so now. Sometimes the despicable treatment involves an inheritance; sometimes it doesn't. Usually what it comes down to is that some upstart kid wants to get out of the house as quickly as possible and with as much as possible to boot. "Can't stand it any longer. I'm eighteen; I'm outta here."

Some of us have had children do that to us; some of us have done that to our parents. Whether we did it or had it done to us, this much is sure: the family can sometimes be a place of agony. It can be an exasperating place for children and a bitter place for parents. We're not talking about blame here; we're talking about reality. Whatever the cause of the family troubles, the reality in most families, I would say, is something like what happened when the younger son showed his father that he didn't care about him as a person—he just wanted his money right away. Thankfully families aren't like this all the time, but most of them are like this some of the time.

What does this story tell us about the mind of Christ? It tells us that he knows all about these situations. He's no dummy. He's not a God on a cloud, off somewhere admiring the sunrise. When our families become like the family in this story, we must remember that Jesus knows what's going on. This story assures us that he knows.

If something like this happened in your family, or is happening—maybe you are the parent who's being abused or you are the kid who's doing it— just remember that Jesus is not surprised. When your family gets nasty, remember that you can talk with Jesus about what's happening. He told a story once about a family just like yours. It's a miserable story, but because of love everything turned out all right.

Lord Jesus, we are ashamed of what goes on in our families sometimes. We know you know all about it and are not surprised. Lord, sometimes we can be so frustrated and bitter that we want to scream. We don't know where to turn or what to do. Thank you for coming to be our Savior even though you know all about us. Give us hope and love on this day, please. In your name, Amen.

Dow Jones Grace

See that you also excel in this grace of giving.

2 Corinthians 8:7

The fact that the first Christians were so reckless with their money is one of the most attractive things about them and one of the scariest. Once the Holy Spirit fell like fire on the church, people began to do strange things with their possessions.

In Acts 4:32-35 we read, "No one claimed that any of his possessions was his own, but they shared everything they had. . . . There were no needy persons among them. For from time to time those who owned lands or houses sold them, brought the money from the sales and put it at the apostles' feet, and it was distributed to anyone as he had need."

Wow. See what I mean by scary? Most of us don't think this way. We play our cards close to our vest. Many of us are Dow Jones people, or NASDAQ, or whatever. We know what's going on. We talk about "our money," "our estate," our this and that, and we complain bitterly when something happens that takes our wealth away.

But if we believe the Bible is God's Word, we cannot ignore passages like this. (See also Mark 10:21 and the closing verses of Acts 2, for example.) The record is there for all to see. Not only did the Holy Spirit loosen clutching hands, allowing the first Christians to surrender their fortunes when he first invaded the church with his power, but this view of money and possessions also accompanied the advance of the gospel as it spread throughout the Roman empire. The apostle Paul wrote the Corinthians about the way this strange "generosity sickness" also fell upon the Macedonians when they first heard the gospel: "Out of the most severe trial, their overflowing joy and their extreme poverty welled up in rich generosity. . . . They gave as much as they were able, and even beyond their ability" (2 Cor. 8:2-3).

As we look at these events from our vantage point, there seems to be a kind of madness in them. It's okay to be impressed by Christ, even to believe in him, we figure, but if such generosity goes with it, we must do something to protect our assets.

But we have to give up that way of thinking. We don't need to protect our assets. Why? Well, we have no assets. We Christians need to realize that. We have nothing that we have not been given, and we have been given it to use in the service of Christ. The moment we pray "Your kingdom come," we surrender everything we have and everything we will ever have. In that instant our kingdoms dissolve, and God's kingdom becomes our focus.

So the apostle tells us that among all the graces we must cultivate, there is this grace too. And as with all graces, it must be something that wells up naturally out of Christ's encounter with our misshapen lives. This is part of the salvation package. God captures us, every bit of us, and he even takes charge of whatever the Dow Jones or anyone or anything else has given us.

What did the Macedonians give when they gave out of their poverty? We cannot know. But what about us? There have never been believers who had more resources than we have today. This means that the great concept that must govern the way I use every gift God has given me is *stewardship*.

I am a steward now. A steward of health, of talent, of material gifts—of everything. All of us are. The first people touched with the Spirit's fire realized that. We who believe today must not blow it. If we do, the reason is likely that we just don't get it. We are not yet submitted fully to the Christ and to his Holy Spirit.

Compared to the first Christians, we are not just rich, but we are sophisticated rich. That's okay. But if our sophistication keeps us from excelling in the grace of giving, it comes from the devil and not from the Spirit of Christ. Scary.

Holy Spirit, touch us with your fire so that we will benefit fully from your presence in our lives. We need you within us, for only then can we live eternally. Take over our lives, we pray, even to the extent that we think of all our possessions as belonging to Christ. May we use them to establish our Father's kingdom, not our own. Amen.

The Hesychasts

"God, have mercy on me, a sinner."
Luke 18:13

The Hesychasts say the Jesus prayer, and they say it over and over again. It goes like this: "Lord Jesus Christ, Son of God, have mercy on me, a sinner." Among the Eastern Orthodox, this prayer is called the prayer of the heart; John of Damascus recommended it in the sixth century.

Before that, Jesus himself recommended it in the story about two men who went into the temple to pray—one of them a despised tax collector, the other a proud Pharisee. The Pharisee got as close to God as he could in the front of the temple; the tax collector stood at the back and prayed, "God, be merciful to me, a sinner." Jesus then explained that the prayer of the despised tax collector, who understood how sinful he was, led to salvation. The other led to something else.

Few of Jesus' teachings are more explicit than the statement he made at the conclusion of this story: "I tell you that this man, rather than the other, went home justified before God. For everyone who exalts himself will be humbled, and he who humbles himself will be exalted" (Luke 18:14).

The unsettling thing about Jesus' clear announcement here—his announcement that salvation religion is characterized by a sense of one's sin—is that so much of North American Christianity disregards this emphasis. An experience of guilt and corruption and confession of sin are often deemphasized in conventional Christianity today. In some cases these things are actively opposed. An article in *Modern Reformation* by Dan Matzat tells how a theologian has said that it is psychologically debilitating to tell people that their sins are the cause of Jesus' crucifixion.

If we want to be true followers of Christ, we must recognize that there are lots of high-profile churches and public religious events today that distort what it means to follow Christ. A heavy emphasis on self-esteem and self-actualization, delivered in an entertainment mode, creates a person who is very different from a person who might say the Jesus prayer repeatedly or who, as the tax collector in Jesus' story, would consider himself unworthy to come near to God at all. It takes a mighty reworking of the Bible to conclude that today's overriding emphasis on feeling good about oneself is authentic Christianity. Self-esteem is what the Pharisee had, and he went home with his sin clinging to him like a rotten odor. The tax collector had no self-esteem whatsoever, and he went home washed clean.

There is no escaping the conclusion that the Christianity of the Bible is a religion that begins in confession of sin and continues in a daily confession of sin. Christianity is the religion that announces that God did everything required to pay for human sin, and it is the religion that requires believers to live each day in a consciousness that they are forgiven sinners first of all and that their need for forgiveness never goes away.

The story of the Pharisee and the tax collector is so important for us because it clearly shows the contrast between true and false religion. These two people were completely dissimilar as they went about their worship. Jesus is not talking here about differences of worship style that appeal to different kinds of people. He is talking about the inner heart condition of the worshiper, the condition that will affect where he stands in the temple and what he says to God. And the seriousness of the issue could not be more absolute. It is clearly possible for a person to worship God formally while on a journey that leads to damnation. The only way to avoid that possibility is to have the consciousness of sin dominating one's heart and worship behavior.

Those who object to Jesus' emphasis here are right when they claim that an alternative will be more popular and pleasing. We continually build mechanisms in our lives that are designed to make us feel good about ourselves. We must abandon each one of them. The simple fact is this: pride and hell go together; humility and salvation go together.

"God, be merciful to me, a sinner." Take this prayer, O Spirit of Christ, and make it mine today and every day. Let it not be for me an empty mantra, but an earnest confession of my corruption and guilt. Gladden my smitten heart with the assurance that your mercy is there for all of us poor sinners who implore you to give it to us. For Jesus' sake, Amen.

Meditation 22

Our Radiant Lives

We . . . are being transformed. . . .

2 Corinthians 3:18

It may well be that my personality has changed over the past several years, but it seems to me that people are a lot less friendly on airplanes than they used to be. Possibly I was more friendly myself twenty years ago, and people would feel they wanted to talk with me. But I don't think it's just me. People on airplanes don't talk to each other much, if at all. Each person seems to be a sort of a capsule sitting next to another capsule, especially during the week when all sorts of businesspeople head off to New York, Toronto, or L.A., pounding away at their laptops.

It would seem, though, that somewhere along the line, in an airplane or on a city bus or even on the street, there should be times when we run across someone who looks like Moses did when he came down from the mountain. I wish I looked more like him than I do.

In Exodus 34 we read that Moses' face was radiant whenever he came away from talking with God. God talked with Moses as a friend talks with a friend (he's the only person the Bible says this about), and when one of their conversations was over, his face was like sunshine. His brother Aaron was uneasy around him. "Please," he said, "won't you put something on your face?" So Moses would wear a veil until he went into God's presence again. If a person gets as close to God as Moses did, it shows on his or her face. Every believer should want to look like Moses, and, as you might know, the apostle Paul closes 2 Corinthians 3 by telling us that when people believe in Jesus Christ, they are transformed too, as Moses was.

Biblical religion is about a transformation of human character that is so profound that it's the contemporary equivalent of what happened to Moses. Because this is true, if you were to look over a random crowd of, say, two hundred people on the street or on an airplane, some of them should stand out from the rest because they would be radiant. Of course, nowadays this would not be a kind of incandescent glow, but it would be a transformation of inner personality that would be so real that it would show on their faces.

It would be so exciting if someday I sat down in a bus or an airplane, looked at the person sitting next to me, and I could say, "Aha! You are one of them. You are living close to Christ. I can see it on your face." Or if someone said to me, "I can see you're living close to Christ. It shows on your face."

It should. It had to show on Moses' face when he had his conversations with God, and the astonishing point the apostle Paul makes in the closing verses of 2 Corinthians 3 is that today New Testament believers have contact with God, just as Moses did. They have this contact because Jesus Christ and the Holy Spirit are so closely united that the apostle could say, "The Lord is the Spirit, and where the Spirit of the Lord is, there is freedom" (3:17). Then Paul says, "And we, who with unveiled faces all reflect the Lord's glory, are being transformed into his likeness with ever-increasing glory, which comes from the Lord, who is the Spirit" (3:18).

Can you imagine what it must have been like when Moses came down from the mountain with the two tablets containing the Ten Commandments in his hand, with his face looking like the sun at noon? "Please, cover up, will you? We cannot bear to look at you," his friends implored him.

Everything that Jesus did pointed toward the goal that we would all be transformed by his glory. Think of this: Moses had contact with God on the mountain; today believers have contact with God when the Holy Spirit comes and lives within them—actually when Jesus comes and lives within them, because "the Lord is the Spirit."

If this is true, we should glow. Just what this means exactly, I don't know. It must have something to do with the way we are inside. But wouldn't you think it would show more on our faces?

Holy Spirit of Jesus Christ, we praise and thank you that it is possible for us today to be even closer to God than Moses was on the mountain. Transform us, we pray, and make us glow through and through and inside out with your glorious presence. We pray in your name, Amen.

Meditation 23

Shooting Stars

What is man that you are mindful of him. . . ?

Psalm 8:4

On the morning of November 17, 1997, I saw the largest shooting star I ever saw in my life. It was 5:40 in the morning, and the east was beginning to show the faintest intimations that the sun would make it up within the next hour; the nearly full moon hung brilliant in the middle of the sky, and the pristine whiteness of snow blanketed rooftops and lawns; the macadam of the street was black as the night that would soon surrender to dawn, and the temperature was about 18 degrees Fahrenheit. I had just begun jogging down the street when a shooting star splashed across the sky right ahead of me, to the north and a bit to the east. It was as if God took a paintbrush and put a wide streak of orange fire across the heavens. I probably imagined it, but it almost seemed that I could hear the hiss of the dying meteor as it crashed into our atmosphere. It looked to me as if it were headed straight for the Sears Tower in Chicago.

I gasped (maybe that was the hiss I heard). And then as I continued jogging, I saw two other shooting stars in quick succession, but they were more the usual kind—pencil-thin streaks of light way off to the west in the distance. The first one, though, was so close that for a brief instant I thought of TWA's Flight 800.

It was an inspiring morning; from then on, the sun gradually took over, and by the time I had finished my jog, it was day. But a feeling of the dominating presence of that first star did not leave me while I was out there, and I thought about how little the sky affects us homebound, urban people. It doesn't really pay to spend much time looking up, with the ambient light of city sprawl robbing the night of its deepest blackness. But when something heavenly shatters you, as that breathtaking meteor shattered me, you realize how it used to be when believers wrote psalms.

Psalm 8 was written by a night person who was often humbled as he pondered the infinity of the heavens. King David wrote, "When I consider your heavens, the work of your fingers, the moon and the stars, which you have set in place, what is man that you are mindful of him, the son of man that you care for him?" (8:3-4).

The fingers of God set the stars in place. The work of his fingers surrounds us and stretches further than the Hubble telescope can see. King David responded to the vast heavens with deepest awe and humbled himself before the Almighty Creator. But his humility was not like the groveling of a pagan before an idol. The Scriptures tell us that the God who made the heavens with his fingers has also written with his finger. Moses descended Mount Sinai with a law written by the finger of God, the same finger that established the universe. And as the great King David acknowledged God's magnificent design and power, he also recognized his destiny as a creature of God "crowned . . . with glory and honor" (8:5).

Surely we are extremely small—each of us. I felt that way that early morning when I nearly stumbled and fell, shocked by the awesome meteor. But the same God who sends meteor showers cascading over our heads provides us with his revelation. Psalm 19, which also responds to the glory of God revealed in the heavens, turns (almost abruptly) from its contemplation of the shimmering universe to the law God wrote with his finger: "The law of the LORD is perfect, reviving the soul. The statutes of the LORD are trustworthy, making wise the simple" (19:7).

A human being, startled by God's meteor being consumed in the earth's atmosphere, may also know that the God who arranges such spectacles has given us mere mortals a magnificent vocation. We may contemplate nature and return our praise; no other part of creation can do that. And we can take up divinely appointed tasks as God's representatives within his creation. "You made him ruler over the works of your hands; you put everything under his feet: all flocks and herds, and the beasts of the field, the birds of the air, and the fish of the sea, all that swim the paths of the seas" (Ps. 8:6-8).

"O LORD, our Lord, how majestic is your name in all the earth!" We join the wonderstruck king of Israel in this exclamation of praise. Thank you for arranging such encounters with your power as meteor showers, often in the early morning. Humble us before you, glorious God, and exalt us too, as we take upon ourselves the magnificent tasks you assign us. We pray in Christ's name, Amen.

The Gehazi Syndrome

Gehazi hurried after Naaman.
2 Kings 5:21

Naaman stands tall among the many enemies of Israel as a noble general. The impression we get is that he was not only a person of unusual military skill but an individual of integrity whose personal qualities were widely recognized. Even the young maiden, captured from the Israelites, respected him and pitied him because of the disease of leprosy that relentlessly ate away at the nerves in his hands and feet and threatened him with an early death. The history of this man's travel to Israel with 750 pounds of silver and 150 pounds of gold along with gifts of clothing in search of healing is well-known among Bible readers.

But we should not dwell only on Naaman's miraculous healing, which occurred when he finally heeded Elisha's puzzling instructions. The record concludes with a detailed account of another disease even more devastating than leprosy. It's the disease that might well be called the Gehazi Syndrome. If leprosy is relatively rare among us, the Gehazi Syndrome is not; it lives on and on and is more destructive than leprosy could ever be. It's the behavior among religious-leadership types whereby they cannot resist the temptation to profit financially whenever possible.

Gehazi's conduct should not be ignored because it is as important for our instruction as is the healing of the noble general. You may recall that Naaman offered Elisha money for all that he had done and that Elisha steadfastly refused it. He did not do the work of the Lord for pay: God's mercy and blessing could not be bought. Elisha wanted nothing of Naaman's silver, gold, or lavish garments.

But Gehazi thought Elisha was nuts. Here was a potential large donor for an important ministry, and Elisha sent him away without even telling him that he would contact him later if an exciting mission project came along. Elisha was hopelessly old-fashioned. Gehazi was the kind of guy you would make director of development for a mission today. Because he saw possibilities here for financial gain, he took off after the cloud of dust in the distance that showed where Naaman and his entourage were on their journey home.

In the mid-1930s one of the founders of the advertising industry said that when you get a crowd of people together, it's a shame not to sell them something. This approach has become the foundation of our free enterprise system: gather crowds, and then sell the crowds to advertisers. This is what television is all about, and sports . . . and much of religion.

The Gehazi Syndrome operates whenever religion is used to gather a crowd of people and sell them something. When you have a church full of people, shouldn't you make some money on them? Especially if it's for a good cause . . . such as the Gehazi retirement fund.

Gehazi, in contrast to Elisha, simply wanted to put everything on a proper financial footing. Elisha had healed Naaman without any consideration of financial gain. Gehazi wanted to correct that "imbalance" and get some silver and some clothing from Naaman. He had to run very fast to do it, and he had to lie. But the bottom line looked a lot better as far as Gehazi was concerned than it would have if he had left it all up to Elisha.

One of the keys to spiritual health today is awareness of the Gehazi Syndrome. Of course, churches need to be supported and religious workers need to be cared for. But the desire to get needed money for all this can quickly move to a level where the Gehazi Syndrome begins to operate. Religious leaders need to be very careful that they do not engage in ministry so that they will be able to raise funds.

And those of us who are ministered to must also be aware of the Gehazi Syndrome. We should not patronize ministries that are actually forms of fund-raising. As soon as the profit motive enters, ministry is contaminated, and everybody loses.

All-seeing God, we confess that there is something of Gehazi in each of us. Deliver us, we pray, from the love of money. Purify the church and those whom you have called to ministry so that they will not run after money but will minister sincerely to all. Give us discernment so that we will not be led astray by money-raising schemes disguised as ministry. In Jesus, Amen.

His Father's Words

"Whatever I say is just what the Father has told me to say."
John 12:50

For those who live a quarter century or more in a single community, it can be uncanny, almost unnerving, to see the similarities between children and their parents. In some cases the child seems to be a virtual clone of the parent. Sometimes when a child is young, you see no similarity whatsoever between the child and the parent, but in another twenty years you may say, "He's just like his father," or, "She's just like her mother."

This is even more true of Jesus and his Father. The great significance of Jesus of Nazareth is that he is, if we may use this word in this sense, a *clone* of his heavenly Father. The book of Hebrews says that the Son of God is the "radiance of God's glory and the exact representation of his being." And Jesus often emphasized that he represented his heavenly Father perfectly.

As we seek for God and long for contact with him, what Jesus says about his closeness to the heavenly Father is extremely important. In the final week before he died, Jesus underscored the significance of his closeness to his Father for the sake of the church's ministry in proclaiming the Word of God. In the tense hours before the crucifixion, Jesus denied that he was the origin of his teaching; it had all come from his Father in heaven. In John 12 Jesus declares that his heavenly Father not only told him *what* to say but also *how* to say it.

In the very shadow of the cross Jesus made statements that not only indicate the connection between his word and the word of his Father but also indicate the abiding importance of the word of God for our lives today. At the close of John 12 Jesus speaks about the judging function of his word. Of those who did not accept his words while he was here (and presumably the same applies to those who do not accept his word today), he says, "That very word which I spoke will condemn him at the last day."

You and I are going to be judged by the words of Jesus. And as he makes that point, he wants us to understand that these words are by no means simply the words of a mortal, sin-cursed person. The words of Jesus are not really the words of Jesus at all; they are the words he learned from the Father. He did not tell us anything but what he learned in the heart of heaven in fellowship with his Father.

Nowadays there's an insatiable hunger for God. All ages have been religious, and this one is no exception; it may even be the most religious age ever. For Christians, however, all the searching for God that goes on outside the Bible is futile. The Bible presents God to us because it presents Jesus. And Jesus presents God to us because everything he said and did he received from his heavenly Father. And, today, when we read about Jesus in the Bible, we are reading a book that was inspired by the Holy Spirit. So when we read Scripture, which is about Jesus from cover to cover, we are being enfolded by the blessed Trinity: Father, Son, and Holy Spirit.

It is surely not enough to view Jesus as a supremely important religious leader. Nor is it enough simply to admire him. When we come into contact with Jesus, we come into contact with everything we need to know about God himself. When we read the Holy Bible, we are in contact with God.

Christianity is the only religion that enables ordinary people to have con-tact with the true God. When we read the Bible, we are not transported into some mystical state. No, we are simply told the words of Christ. And these words do not originate from human will any more than Jesus himself did. When we hear the words of Jesus, we hear the very words of God himself. And these words bring God's judgment into our lives.

Often we encourage one another to read the Bible, and that's good to do. Often we work hard at distributing the Bible to those who do not have it, and that's good to do. But we must never forget that we are encouraging them to contact the Word that judges. Nothing is more important than hearing the Word of God and believing it. Rejecting it is fatal.

God the Father, thank you for revealing what is on your heart by sending Jesus, your Son, to us. Help us to pay the closest attention possible to our Savior and to remember always that as we do that, we are having contact with you, our heavenly Father. Father, Son, and Holy Spirit, surround us with your love and mercy this day. We pray in Christ's name, Amen.

Incredible Comfort

Comfort, comfort my people, says your God.

Isaiah 40:1

Isaiah 40:1 is well known among those who read the Bible; for many of us, it is difficult to separate the biblical text from Handel's *Messiah*—just reading the words here in Isaiah, we hear the haunting, plaintive song of the tenor who draws them out and lets them fall soothingly on our ears. But today let's try to focus on when these words were first written and spoken and read.

Isaiah, the most political of the prophets, is speaking to Jerusalem and announcing a brilliant future. As he delivered the words of Isaiah 40, he must have wondered himself what had come over him. There was nothing in the circumstances around him that supported what he was speaking of. Nothing. The city was in a shambles. That Isaiah wrote this when he did is incredible. That he could speak of comfort to a city doomed to be destroyed because of its own wretched folly is unbelievable.

We must look at this strange situation because it will help us receive the comfort of God in our distressed age and, as we often must, in our own difficult experiences. If you ever want to feel the jarring force of Isaiah's words, take the time to read 1 and 2 Kings and the books written by the chronicler. These books depict the unspeakable degradation of the people of God.

Isaiah most likely penned these words during the reign of Manasseh, the most wicked of the kings of Judah—and one of the worst in all Israel. Of him, the writer of 2 Kings says, "Manasseh led [the people] astray, so that they did more evil than the nations the Lord had destroyed before the Israelites" (21:9). This king, who ruled longer than any other, systematically uprooted whatever was left of the true worship of God and set up altars to false gods right in the Jerusalem temple. He sacrificed his own son by passing him through the fire. Never had the holy city been so devastated physically, morally, and spiritually. Within a few decades Judah would follow hapless Israel into captivity, and their punishment would be richly deserved. "Surely these things happened to Judah according to the LORD's command, in order to remove them from his presence because of the sins of Manasseh and all he had done" (24:3).

We who listen to Isaiah's call for comfort in a concert hall must be reminded of the desolation to which this call first came. For us who know the Bible's full story, the fact that Isaiah 40 was written in such a desolate age can be a magnificent consolation. We who often bemoan the degradation that has overtaken our society—in some cases even the church itself—must realize that our times are not unique. It is doubtful whether the depth of rebellion against God today is much different from the fullness of Manasseh's horrific degeneration.

People of God, hear the word of Isaiah once again!

We should say this to one another. As we read the entire chapter of Isaiah 40, which is so rich with encouragement, it lifts our hearts in our troubled times. It's so easy to become discouraged by the seemingly overwhelming power of evil that creeps beneath the doors of our homes and invades our most private of lives with violence and licentiousness. The evil ideas that float through the air we breathe make us cringe. We are appalled that people are corrupted from the time they are toddlers. It seems at times that all is lost.

But no, God calls his people to rise up and trust him. The chapter closes, as you may know, with the reminder that God, after all, is "the everlasting God" who "will not grow tired or weary" (Isa. 40:28). And it is God's unconquerable strength that enfolds and empowers his children. Within the hearts and faltering limbs of the weak, God will enkindle new power.

Today again it seems as if Manasseh is on the throne. Even what we would expect to be pure often displays a befouling corruption. But just when it seems as if all hope has fled, the voice of the Almighty sounds anew, and we are comforted.

Comfort us, Almighty God, as we survey the shambles of this rebellious age and seek to learn our duty. Help us understand that no earthly force can ever be superior to your power. Visit our weary lives with your Holy Spirit and equip us to walk and run and rise up to honor you in our small lives. We know this is possible because of Christ. In his name, Amen.

This Blessed Book

"I will write on them. . . ."

Exodus 34:1

If you read the Bible only occasionally, you'll have to excuse those of us who read it all the time, again and again. You'll have to excuse us for the awe we have of this book. The more we read it, the more we are awestruck. Though bound in a single volume we can hold in our hand, the Bible is more impressive than all of creation.

Take the very first words of the Bible, for example, words that have come to us through an action that surpasses *inspiration*, the process we usually refer to when we try to speak of the Bible's origin. Yes, it is true: the very first words of the Bible were not inspired.

And what are these first words? Not Genesis 1:1. The description of God's creation of the universe and of humankind and the record of our fall into sin became a part of the sacred record later under Moses' direction through inspiration. We do not know precisely how Genesis was placed within the sacred record. In any case, Genesis 1:1 is not the first word of sacred Scripture delivered to Moses. The words of the Law of God are the first.

And God wrote the words of his law himself; they are not inspired. When the commandments were initially given on the tablets of stone, Exodus 31 concludes the record of that event by saying: "When the Lord finished speaking to Moses on Mount Sinai, he gave him the two tablets of the Testimony, the tablets of stone inscribed by the finger of God."

Those tablets were destroyed when Moses threw them down in anger upon seeing the people worshiping the golden calf. But later, when Moses returned to God, God said he would write the words once more: "Chisel out two stone tablets like the first ones, and I will write on them the words that were on the first tablets, which you broke."

It's true that we also read that Moses was involved in placing the Ten Commandments on this second set of tablets (Ex. 34:28). Yet the impression we are left with is that God wrote these first words of Scripture himself, with his own finger (31:18).

For those who are acquainted with theories that have reduced the Bible to merely another expression of the evolutionary development of religious consciousness, the words that speak of God's direct inscription of the Ten Commandments seem quaint at best. They seem unworthy of citizens of the computer age. To be sure, there's a strong temptation to insist that a natural explanation lies behind these words. But we must not yield to it. The Bible is like no other book. It is not even a book in the conventional sense. It is the message we have from God, written on tablets of stone, on papyrus and leather, now on paper and on CD-ROM. It is God's Word. Yes, there is such a thing in this world; there is something that can be called God's Word.

Some people insist it is wrong to revere a book. Come now—really? Have you ever been a soldier far from home, possibly dreadfully afraid that you would never see your darling again? Her letters—what did they mean to you? That attachment is something that occurs simply between human beings—lovers, to be sure—but still human. There's no explanation for this book, which was written over a seventeen-hundred-year span by human authors who for the most part never saw each other face to face, and yet it presents a unified message of divinity and humanity connected in the drama of salvation. The Bible is a miracle, as surely as Christ's resurrection is a miracle, though it lies by our sickbed as any other book would. Surely we may not make it an idol, but may we not revere this blessed presence in our lives?

To be sure, we must be careful with our reverence. The pages and the black and sometimes scarlet letters upon them cannot save. As such, they are as inert as helium. But the message they convey comes straight from heaven's deepest mystery, from the very heart of God. Those who read it always and who never cease learning its message feel God's very presence as they meet him in Jesus Christ and receive the Spirit of the Living God.

There is room for reverence when we speak of such a book.

Thank you, Lord God, for giving us the Bible. Forgive us if we say things about it that are not quite accurate; if we do that, it's because we cannot understand exactly how it all happened. But we know that it was your grace that brought it to us, grace that shows us how to live, grace that saves us when we fail, grace that empowers us as we obey. Amen.

Job

"The LORD gave and the LORD has taken away; may the name of the LORD be praised."

Job 1:21

The book of Job is one of the most puzzling books in the Bible. The issue it deals with is so profound and real that we leave it shaking our heads. Here is the account of a reversal of fortune that came swiftly and reduced a rich, powerful man to despair. It happens all the time.

Theoretically most of us would admit that trouble and suffering can have their good side. They can cause us to slow down and set us thinking about important things. But when trouble is nothing more than a fierce horror, there is no learning from it anymore. It's just awful. You want to put your face in your hands and bawl, but no tears come—you've cried them all away.

Job's calamity was so devastating because it followed incomparable prosperity. The river had been flowing in the right direction for so long that Job had become "the greatest man among all the people of the East." Job was a thoroughly good man, but—good or not—when everything turns around, when you lose your children, your wealth, your health—everything—you're shattered.

Only a spiritual giant could say, as Job did, that God had given him everything and that God had taken it away and that God should be praised. Don't assume you've ever met anyone quite this great; surely none of us comes close. Job makes this magnificent statement in the first chapter of this book, and he makes another, similar statement in chapter 2: "Shall we accept good from God, and not trouble?" (2:10). It's amazing that in his loss of wealth, health, and most of his family, Job never loses his faith in God.

There are rich Christians who go through something like Job's circumstances nowadays—they have been riding high, and they have always acknowledged that the prosperity they enjoyed came from God. But now they are pinching pennies, slinking around so that they will not meet their old friends. There are people who have enjoyed marvelous health, and they have always acknowledged that God was the giver. But now they have become stammering, stumbling victims of a merciless disease—they can't even make it to the john. Should they now acknowledge that God has given this to them too? What do they do now?

When God takes our treasure from us, what do we do? When he takes the basic necessities of a good life away, what do we do? When God leaves us quivering, pain-racked skeletons of humanity, what do we do?

I couldn't begin to answer these questions for anyone who is in such a desolate state. But the book of Job helps somewhat, puzzling as it is. It tells us that our miseries are related in some way to a cosmic interplay between God and Satan. We must be careful that we do not read too much into the conversation recorded in the book of Job between God and Satan, but surely we are being told, are we not, that the devil is in our suffering somewhere. It happens because of his treacherous desire to put us through hell so that our faith will vanish.

And sometimes it seems as if it might. When we must express our faith at the nadir of tragedy, we discover that it does not have quite the shape it had when we were on the receiving end of God's blessings. We still believe, but our faces are contorted with questions as we glance furtively heavenward. "Lord, why? Please, why are you doing this to me?"

The book of Job closes with a humbled man acknowledging that the ways of God are beyond our fathoming. We must acknowledge that God is God and that we are tangled in a mysterious interplay of good and evil. No answer is finally satisfying for us while we are in this state. And so we bow before the Lord; our heavy heads drop forward, and we are silent.

And then we see him—Jesus. Here is the crucified Christ right in this miserable mess with us. And Jesus will yet take us through to glory. I know he will. That's all I know. That's all. And that has to be enough.

O Lord, you are the one who gives, and you are the one who takes away; may your holy name be praised. Help us praise you when, for whatever reason, you set us on the ash heap. Lord, it can be really terrible down here where we live. Deliver us. Lift us up and restore us. Turn our eyes to you and help us to believe that all of this makes divine sense. In Jesus' name, Amen.

His Religion and Ours

When the ten heard about this, they were indignant. . . .
Matthew 20:24

Of course Jesus' disciples were ticked, but not for the right reasons. It wasn't that they had it right and that Salome and her sons had it wrong. They all had it wrong. The disciples were so angry because they realized that James and John had gotten ahead of them.

Salome, the mother of James and John, was a very intelligent woman. She was a believer in Christ, as were her sons and the other disciples. When she approached Jesus with her question, Jesus was already on his way to Jerusalem to face the cross; if the sequence of Matthew's gospel reflects the actual sequence, Jesus had just told all of them that he was going to be crucified. Salome, however, believed that Jesus would be exalted one day as King of kings, ruler of the kingdom above all others. Her faith was strong, visionary, and accurate. The trouble was that it was mixed with the same elements that corrupt our faith today.

Honor, power—something deep inside us makes us crave them and connive to get them. Salome and her sons were willing to risk the anger of the others to gain honor and power. "Please, let my sons flank you on your throne, Lord."

Human nature doesn't change. Think of this ultrareligious age we are living in now. Deeply religious people, with a great faith in Christ, haven't gotten over wanting to be exalted with him. Christ's people will ultimately be exalted with him, but in this age we are not talking about "ultimately"; we are talking about now. When Christ's followers are finally exalted in glory, they will also be fully sanctified, and their pride and their passionate desire for power will have been destroyed.

Now it's different. Now religion offers its own perks. There are stretch limousines, the excitement of travel, recognition, hobnobbing with heads of state, lots of money. There is power here; large organizations go one way or another depending on the whim of a single individual.

And if you are not positioned to soar nationally or internationally, there's always the local church with its opportunities for exercising power. Religion and power go together. Always have. Always will.

So Salome and her sons approached Jesus Christ. It is comforting to observe how kindly he responded. Coming immediately after his own announcement of his upcoming cruel death, he would have been justified in responding with shock and sharp reprimand. But no. Jesus knew their hearts, and he knows ours. We believe in him; we even trust him, but we cannot shake off our selfishness. "While we were still sinners, Christ died for us" (Rom. 5:8)—he knew how small and mean we are inside; he knew how impossible it is for us simply to believe in him, with no thought of self, no thought of what we will get out of it.

Denominational labels, family religious history—nothing will insure that our faith in Christ is pure. What it will take for us to be purified is that we focus on Christ alone. When we do, he tells us that following him properly has nothing to do with exaltation, nor with power. Look at him and see that true religion is about being Christlike—and that means servanthood.

Jesus deals gently with Salome and her two sons and with the ten other disciples who were incensed for the wrong reasons. All thirteen of them were the same; the ten were upset because they hadn't talked to Jesus about their futures earlier—maybe they felt frustrated because they didn't have their mothers with them to help. Who knows? Jesus told these confused believers that true religion is absolutely different from what they had in mind.

As I hear the words of Jesus conveyed across the centuries, I must remember that this is not just one man talking to another. This is God revealing the essence of true religion. Being willing to serve is the essence of true religion because God has become a servant. God is like this. And he invites us to be like him. He wants us to forget about thrones and think about serving. This is the opposite of what I am by nature. Is it possible that God's Holy Spirit could rehabilitate me today?

Lord Jesus, I need to be rehabilitated. We tremble and hang our heads in shame as we think of what you find when you look into our selfish hearts. Please forgive us for striving for recognition and power, and give us the gentle spirit of servanthood. Thank you for the divine example you have given. Thank you for saving us sinners by giving your very life for us. Amen.

A Good Androgyny

"[He] has already committed adultery . . . in his heart."
Matthew 5:28

Most male Christians have pondered Jesus' teaching about adultery and wondered how it applied to them. Some have erroneously concluded that since they have done the deed already in their heart, they might as well go all the way. Others, who have valued their purity, have suspected that because of their occasional lust they were as guilty as any philanderer, and they've been miserable.

When you try to figure this out, it's worth remembering that Jesus approached murder the same way; he identified murder as including behavior that fell short of actually pulling the trigger. Slander and ridicule are already murderous, he said. Both adultery and murder are attitude sins. And not only men but also women have these sinful attitudes.

There have probably never been more adulterers than there are now. The entertainment industry has always featured eroticism designed to ignite lust. There are live shows and television and movie fare that make such entertainment available in the home. And degenerate, degrading, filthy pornography is only a double click away for anyone with access to the Internet.

Along with all of this is omnipresent advertising that features people in various stages of undress. It's everywhere—Marshall Field's parades women in their underthings on page two of the daily newspaper. Jockey underwear ads feature men and women in tight-fitting briefs and other undergarments. What's a poor soul who wants to maintain his or her purity to do? If Jesus is serious, and you can bet he is (just read the context in which he talks about heart-adultery), lots of us have a problem.

Is there a way out of this? There is.

Think about what makes adultery vicious. Is the arousal that accompanies adultery evil in itself? It can be. But that's not the essence of this sin. Adultery is evil because it deprives another person of his or her personhood. The adulterer, whether by heart-adultery or the full-blown act, participates in the ruination of a precious human being. Bearing this in mind, we recognize that a good androgyny can help.

Androgyny is often wrong; it can be the refusal to recognize that men and women are different. New Age ideas are often androgynous. So are some radical feminist ideas. But for Christians who want to rise above their natural lust, a good androgyny can save their virtue.

We must learn to look at all people, men and women, as persons first of all. Persons, people, come in two styles or packages. Some of them are packaged female, and some male. But whatever the package, each person is a person, created in the image of God, with dignity and high responsibility. Men must learn to look at all women as people first of all, and the same goes for women with regard to men, understanding that all of us have obligations to each other as persons.

Writing to a young preacher, the apostle Paul told him he should treat younger women as sisters. Very simple. He was not to treat them in terms of their sexuality but in terms of the way they fit into the society of that day.

Pornography is viciously evil because it teaches those who use it to view other people in terms of their sexuality. We may not think of people that way; we must think of them as persons. And pornography is evil because it causes those who are part of producing it to think of themselves in terms of their sexuality. They must think of themselves as persons.

Adultery is primarily a sin of the inner self. When Jesus says that it can be committed within the heart, he is not using a figure of speech. Heart-adultery is viciously evil because it denies another person's personhood.

People who seriously want to be pure will remove all temptation to lust from their environment. And they will train themselves to look at everyone they meet as a person first of all. Such training does not come easily, but if diligently pursued it results in transformed persons who are pure through and through.

Lord Jesus, you see into our very hearts. Help us to realize the depths of our sin. Help us to be honest with you and with others and ourselves. Cleanse us, O Lord, and make us pure within. Enable us to greet and treat all the people we meet as persons, whoever they may be. We pray in your name, Amen.

Washed

But you were washed. . . .
1 Corinthians 6:11

They tell us the crime rate is going down in our big cities. But there is still enough murder, mayhem, and rape to sell Pontiacs on the late-night news. Those who want to end their day on that note will not be disappointed.

Perhaps we should be thankful that wickedness still makes news—if it were as acceptable as a garden show and not newsworthy anymore, we would be even worse off. And yet some of it has become acceptable. The apostle Paul lists a number of human perversities in his letters (for example, 1 Cor. 6:9-10) and many of those are seen as okay now, at least in some circles.

The Bible is supposed to be inspirational, but long stretches of it are not, in the sense we usually refer to as inspirational. It is hardly like one of Mary Steiner Rice's poems, or even one of Robert Frost's. The Old Testament presents an array of stumbling saints, heroes of faith who occasionally acted like everybody else. Take war, for example, which is always cruel—it was waged with a merciless horror, as when David took Moabite captives and killed two thirds of them. Those who insist that human nature is good will not find proof of that in the holy Scriptures.

"That is what some of you were," the apostle reminds the Corinthians in the midst of his solemn call to get with the program and start behaving the way saints should. He calls the congregation in Corinth to a new level of wholesome living by declaring the happy message of righteous possibility. True, human nature is wretchedly perverse, but believers don't have to be that way.

For all its realism about us, the Scriptures are stunningly and gloriously happy because they announce the possibility of rising above our sinful nature. For believers in Christ, what is deviant and corrupting can be put in the past. That's the way you *were*, good friend. "But you were washed, you were sanctified, you were justified in the name of the Lord Jesus Christ and by the Spirit of our God." Is there a sentence more joy-filled, more liberating than this one?

Washed, sanctified, justified—go figure. *Washed* reminds us that through Jesus Christ those who have been made dirty by sinfulness have the dirt removed. There are days when the flashbacks to another time or another place can intrude and leave you staring into the middle distance. *Did I really do that?* Coming back from a night in the village, a soldier on Okinawa told his buddies about his sordid escapades. They laughed and hooted. Then he added, suddenly serious, "And I liked it." Later, coming from the shower, he muttered, "I just can't get clean." God washes, and he uses the blood of his Son, Jesus, to do it.

Believers are *sanctified* too. Beyond the washing is the killing of impulses that compel sin. The apostle Paul writes about this elsewhere in terms of people dying to sin. There are some things that never tempt us because it's as if we're dead to those things. Many have never been tempted to run a marathon, for example, or to play golf; it's as if they are dead when someone suggests these things in their presence. Thankfully, it can become that way with sin. The name of Jesus is what accomplishes this killing, and the Spirit of God is who does it.

And *justified*—that's the ultimate possibility for people who were sexually immoral, idolaters, adulterers, male prostitutes, homosexual offenders, thieves, drunkards, slanderers, or swindlers, as Paul pegs them (and surely something here describes each of us). Through the name of Jesus and the Spirit of our God, behavior like this can be erased from the record of all who flee to Jesus for their salvation.

There is only one response to all this: *Hallelujah!*

Holy God, help us to live as men and women who have been washed, sanctified, and justified. Cleanse us, kill the evil inclinations within, and look upon us as people whose record has been made clean through the cross of Christ. Father, Son, and Holy Spirit, we need all you have done and all you now do if we are to live purely today. Please help us. In Jesus' name, Amen.

Brother Jabez

Jabez was more honorable than his brothers.
I Chronicles 4:9

Once when I was talking with the late Ray Dillard, our conversation got around to which part of the Bible was his favorite. He said the books of Chronicles were his. Then he explained that for him the careful genealogies found there confirmed the love of God for people like us.

Ray Dillard could understand those genealogies better than most of us— they were his specialty when he was a professor of Old Testament theology at Westminster Seminary in Philadelphia. But all of us do well to read those lists occasionally. Among all the persons described there, we will find brother Jabez. He was a man who prayed, and he prayed for the right thing.

For the most part the lists of names roll along with little interruption as the Chronicles open until, suddenly, the writer (it may have been Ezra) gets to Jabez of the tribe of Judah. At this point the writer stops everything he is doing and takes a moment to single out this remarkable man. His birth had become fairly well known because of the ordeal his mother had gone through to bring him into the world, and he, survivor of that trauma, had become famous as an especially prayerful man, who habitually placed all of life before God in prayer and enjoyed many unusual answers to his supplications.

The New International Version presents Jabez's story in terms of pain, as if his mother delivered him in pain and he asked to be delivered from pain in his own experience. But the two words translated as *pain* are different here: his mother's has more to do with sorrow, and his has more to do with evil. He prayed for the usual things like the expansion of territory, which was a common interest in his day as well as in ours, and also for deliverance from evil.

Now, what's the reason for pointing out Jabez in this way? Why among all who traipse across the opening chapters of Chronicles does this man stand among the few who are singled out?

For one thing, this book was written for the Jewish people who had returned from exile, and it was meant to reaffirm the importance of the tribe of Judah, from which the Messiah would surely come. Jabez emerges as a person who shows by his godly life that piety has not been absent from this important tribe even in its darkest hour. Jabez's life view seems to have been characterized by a certain sensitivity brought about by his awareness of how close he had come to perishing at birth. He apparently sensed that God had put him on this earth through a special provision of his care. He could not shake off that conviction.

Second, the spotlight falls on Jabez because it was prayer that made him notable. It is not only Jabez who is brought within the circle of light here, but also prayer itself. We learn here that in addition to the special prayers the priests were called to offer for the people, there were the ordinary prayers of the pious children of Abraham.

And, third, if we take the word in Jabez's prayer to mean "evil" instead of "pain," there is a remarkable similarity between the prayer of Jabez and the perfect prayer Christ taught us. Jabez of course was interested in his territory, his house and garden plot, the land he and his clan lived on—so he prayed for these. But when he prayed for deliverance from evil, he prayed in a way similar to the closing of the Lord's Prayer: "Deliver us from evil" (Matt. 6:13). Jesus ended his prayer by looking at the degenerate world that surrounded his people and by urging them to pray for deliverance.

Jabez did exactly that, centuries before Christ was born, and the chronicler announces that God answered his prayer. We who pray today in Christ's good name, then, take our place beside our brother Jabez. The chronicler paused to make sure we learned about him, and today we pause to marvel that like Jabez we still can pray for ordinary things such as territory and for one of the most important things of all: deliverance from evil.

Almighty and most merciful God, today we take our stand beside our brother Jabez. We have the same concerns he had. We too need to have adequate shelter and "territory." Please provide it. And, pure and holy God, you see the evil on every side of us. Deliver us, we pray, from all this wretchedness, and make us holy in your presence. Through Christ, Amen.

The Betrayer's Hand

"[His] hand . . . is with mine on the table."
Luke 22:21

President Franklin D. Roosevelt declared that December 7, 1941, would forever live in infamy. On that day, the Japanese bombed Pearl Harbor, killing twenty-four hundred Americans and wounding twelve hundred. When it happened, we all believed no one would ever forget that treacherous attack. But many never give it a thought when, on December 7, they drive their Lexuses and minivans off to work.

Humankind's treachery is a centuries-long stain that befouls our history. But the treachery described by Dr. Luke in his gospel account of the Last Supper is unquestionably the most horrifying example of perfidy that has ever occurred. Luke carefully lays down the sordid details. If we really empathized with what is portrayed here, we would excuse ourselves from listening to the reading and look for a place to vomit.

At first glance, it appears to be an editorial oversight that this careful historian announced, "When the hour came, Jesus and his apostles reclined at the table." The honorific title *apostle* should not be applied to the betrayer, we figure, but there it stands. Judas was still part of the apostolic band. We must not forget that this Passover/Lord's Supper feast was a distinctively "churchly" meeting.

Jesus was at the peak of his messianic consciousness and ability. The apostle John tells us, "He did not need man's testimony about man, for he knew what was in a man" (John 2:25). Frequently he would engage people in conversation about their thoughts, though no one had voiced them. He knew. He knew. And on that day in the upper room, he knew that his archenemy Satan had entered into Judas's heart and that Judas had fallen.

What a sight it must have been for Jesus as he gazed around that room! At some point during that final meeting with all twelve apostles he had actually washed their feet—Judas's too. Now he looked at them and saw within their hearts. There must have been some divine printout of their confusion and indwelling selfishness that, even then, could not keep them from disputing who of them would be greatest.

So he gave them the elements of the supper that still endures in sacramental form within his church. "This is my body," he said solemnly, and then, "This cup is the new covenant in my blood. . . ." His hands moved in the characteristic fashion he used when he broke food and distributed it. And their hands reached out and received the holy morsels and cradled the cup as they drank the covenantal wine. He saw their hands move, one by one, and he saw Judas's hand fall back upon the table after the betrayer had received the sacred elements. He saw all their hearts, but he spoke of that hand.

This is the day that will live forever in infamy. Every military treachery pales into insignificance compared to what happened when hell and heaven faced each other at that first communion. Here was the church in its most solemn moment, but one of the persons there had surrendered to the powers of darkness. Jesus saw all this with a clarity we cannot begin to imagine.

Often we are surprised and disappointed when the church displays how tainted it can be by human treachery. Surely within the church there are innumerable occasions for repentance and confession. Sorrow-filled we must surely be—but surprised, never. The one who betrayed our Lord with a kiss had sat with him. Their hands had been together on the table. From the ranks of the apostolic band came a man of unspeakable depravity.

We must not expect too much of the earthly church. Today it is as needful of redemption as it ever was. There are many who sin against Christ, but only those who have been made part of the church can betray him. And now, when the holy Supper is served yet again, Christ again sees the hands of those who circle the sacramental table. Some of those hands, still today, are hands of betrayers. And sometimes, when he sees deep within my heart and when he examines my daily record, would he also have to say of me, "I see the hand of a betrayer once again"?

Lord Jesus Christ, thank you for never turning aside from the cross, even when you saw just how depraved we can be. Look at your church today, so often disfigured by strife. Through your all-powerful Spirit, O Christ, keep us from betraying you. Help us withstand the countless pressures to deny you. See our hands at your table and have mercy on us, we pray. In your name, Amen.

My Mountain Goats

"Do you know when the mountain goats give birth?"

Job 39:1

Well, I, uh . . . I must confess, Lord, I don't know a thing about mountain goats. And you would have to ask my brother about what happens when a "doe bears her fawn" (Job 39:1)—he watches deer a lot more than I do. In fact, I, a pathetic city dweller, would have to say that all the questions you asked Job after his horrible ordeal are quite beyond me. Ostriches? Uh, uh. I've only seen a couple of them in my life.

Questions like these come up near the end of a book about suffering in which the wretch who suffers does not hesitate to ask the most unsettling question human beings can ever ask about their misery: God, tell me, why are you doing this to me? Why are you shooting your arrows into my life? You know I am innocent. You know that. Why are you doing this to me? So Job spoke to God, and his cringing uncertainties were a bitter contrast to his four friends' stolid dogmas that were supposed to comfort him.

When God finally spoke to Job, he didn't answer his whys, but he enabled Job to see himself as a mysterious little part of God's overwhelmingly marvelous creation. And if I were in misery, God would not talk to me about mountain goats; he would talk to me about robins. I know robins.

When a nest appeared on a ledge just above eye level two feet from my front door on a cruelly cold spring day, I figured a robin had swallowed too much insecticide and had gone nutty. And when the azure eggs appeared, I regretted not having brushed the nest off its precarious perch; that, at least, would have encouraged the mother robin to go elsewhere. Now I would have to witness the inevitable tragedy, for nothing good could ever come of this.

How wrong I was! She sat there, fluffed big and round, eyeing those who entered our front door with steely courage. And then one day the nest was full of little creatures, beaks bigger than the rest of their ugly, fuzzy, throbbing flesh. A new despair gripped me. Now I would have to witness these little things waste away to nothing.

But no. They grew almost as I watched them. Within a week I could tell that they were going to make it. On the morning that I wrote these words, all three of the hatchlings huddled for the first time on the ledge outside the nest. They saw me and were curious. Their fuzz was now gone, and full feathers revealed that they would fly within a day or so. I have never, ever seen anything like this before. These are my mountain goats.

Nature humbles us—the nature God has made. Job, with all his questions flung toward heaven's throne, was reminded of the grand processes of nature, of mountain goats and bear and deer and ostriches and mammals of the ocean. Don't forget, little man, that you are actually part of all this yourself. And God is God. The God who has created all the wonders of nature has also created you. And he is in charge.

Three trembling robins huddling on a ledge by my front door have humbled me. Surely we must let the world that is alive with the fire of God humble us all. The ordinary processes that bring a little bird out of an azure egg leave us baffled. And we know that there was a time when we were not here. And now we are here. And the day will come when we are gone.

Thank God for our mountain goats, whatever shape they take. And today we can thank him for far more than mountain goats. We now know more than Job could have known in his day. We have learned that the greatest wonder of God is his love. The same God who placed that exquisite parable of nature at my front door has shown us his loving heart. It is so full of love that he gave us his most precious Son on the cross for our eternal life.

When we, poor souls, must sometimes suffer as Job did, God comes to us and asks us not only about mountain goats, but also, "Do you understand what happened at the cross? Do you understand my love?"

O, dear God, we do not understand your love. The chronic illnesses that plague us, the cruel diseases that steal our strength, the intrusion of devastating accidents—all of these torture us with questions about you. Humble us, O Lord, so that when we are baffled by calamity, we will remember that the greatest mystery is the mystery of your love in Jesus. Amen.

The Bitter Root

See to it that . . . no bitter root grows up. . . .
Hebrews 12:15

The journey may be a splendid one (when you look at everything right), but things happen that can make the splendor disappear as does the sun in a summer storm. Accident, sickness, financial loss, disgrace, professional failure—no life is immune to these. And when any of them strikes, or if they strike in merciless combination, you discover the root of bitterness.

Bitterness can sneak up on a person who never felt it before. The person may have had setbacks in her life—but nothing she couldn't handle, nothing she couldn't rise above. Sometimes just a good night's rest would help. And after a good cup of hazelnut coffee first thing in the morning, she could go on to other things, and the glitch would recede.

But other times the most dreadful things can happen. As Job said, "What I feared has come upon me; what I dreaded has happened to me" (3:25). We call it a worst-case scenario. We imagine the worst, but we really don't expect it. And yet the worst can happen.

Breast cancer can sneak up and cause bitterness, and, strangely, it can sometimes do this to husbands more than to their wives. Getting cheated out of one's house and fortune can bring on bitterness, and, strangely, sometimes it can do this to wives more than to husbands. You never know how calamity will affect people. But it does affect them, and the worst effect is bitterness.

In the throes of bitterness we discover the truth about ourselves. We learn how thin the veneer of happiness and cheer actually is. We learn how thready our faith really is. "Climb, climb up sunshine mountain, heavenly breezes blow. . . ." Bah, humbug. The truth about ourselves is not pretty.

In the book of Hebrews, bitterness is assailed not only because of what it does to our fragile moods but also because of what it does to community. You come away from Hebrews 12 with the impression that a lack of holiness, missing the point of grace, and fertilizing the root of bitterness all make community centrifugal. They make it fly apart. Bitter people throw courtesy to the winds and say cruel things to each other.

Take Job's wife after he lost his health, his wealth, and all his children. "You're nuts," she said to him. "How can you just sit there after what has happened and not even cuss?" It was incomprehensible to her, and she came right out and told him to curse God (2:9). Because she was bitter. And later Job became just about as bitter as she was, and some of what he said to God came as close to cursing as you can get without actually taking the holy Name in vain. Bitterness drives people apart, and it drives people and God apart.

What should we do when we become bitter?

First we have to recognize our bitterness. It's possible for people to be overrun by all sorts of wretched emotions—hatred, distrust, depression—and not realize that their real problem is bitterness. They are reacting to one or more events that make them mad, mad, mad—and they are not accustomed to thinking of themselves as people who get that way. What we need to do is take ourselves to a quiet place and face up to the nest of vipers inside us.

Then we have to be honest about what our bitterness is doing to us and to others. Look around, bitter boy, bitter girl, and see all the people you are alienated from because of your bitterness. Look what's happening to you. Realize that it's going to keep happening if you don't change. And you have to change—you have to. Search out a Christian friend or counselor who can help you in this.

Then, I guess, what we have to do is read Hebrews 12 over and over again. Until it sinks in. That's the chapter that has this sentence in it: "Let us fix our eyes on Jesus." Yes, let us do that. When we do that, we meet the man who saw the cross ahead of him and who understood how woefully unjust it all was. He saw the glory beyond it. So he went ahead and did what he had to do. And he wasn't bitter. He was loving.

God wants me to love my enemies. He wants me to love those who have ruined my life. He doesn't want me to be bitter. And because I know that, I know he'll help me get over it. It will take a miracle. Of course. But God can do that. Only he can.

Lord Jesus, help me remember what you experienced. HELP ME REMEMBER! Not just know it, with my head, but remember it at all times. Lord, I want always to remember your steadfast love in the face of a suffering that could have made you so bitter that you could have abandoned us all. But you didn't do that. Thank you, Jesus. Please take my bitterness away. Amen.

Meditation 36

He Will Do Right

"Will not the Judge of all the earth do right?"
Genesis 18:25

You don't have to go to seminary to figure out that God has something to do with everything that is going on. When life is going very well, you don't have a problem with that. But when your child has a fever and you have to go to work and there is no one else to care for him, you start to wonder what God is up to. If you come to the conclusion that God is in charge of everything but he cannot be relied on, or, even worse, that he gets a perverse enjoyment out of seeing us squirm, life becomes unbearable, and you become a cynic.

When we think of God's relation to human life, there are few biblical passages that yield more help than the record of Abraham's conversation with God about "the cities of the plain" (Gen. 13:12). The Old Testament reveals that there comes a time when God can no longer put up with human rebellion. The Bible tells us that just prior to the universal flood, God was enormously angry with humanity; he even regretted that he had made the human race. And in connection with the cities of the plain, the most infamous being Sodom, God had had enough; he had to destroy them. The problem, though, was that right in the middle of that city lived Abraham's nephew, whose family had been thoroughly corrupted by the city. So God discussed with Abraham what was going to happen.

That God would even do this leaves us wordless—surely he had no obligation to Abraham. That the conversation is recorded in such detail is also astonishing. And perhaps most astonishing of all is the boldness of Abraham, the "father of believers," who acted as a mediator.

The entire episode assures us that God, who is "the Judge of all the earth," will certainly do right. Abraham raises the issue with a question that is both rhetorical and yet requires an answer. And to this question God gives an answer that, while somewhat mysterious, is most assuredly an answer. He indicates that he most certainly will do right.

As I have traced the Hebrew word for "right" with my own feeble knowledge of the language, I have discovered that this particular word is used mostly in the Old Testament in connection with the rights of people. It is not the same word we use to mean "righteousness"; it is not the same word we use to refer to abstract justice. It refers to human beings as they are dealt with by the Judge of all the earth. God sees what we do, and he knows why we do it. He reacts to what we do. And when human beings defy God, they will be punished.

While it is true that God does not give a direct answer to Abraham's question "Will not the Judge of all the earth do right?" he actually does answer it as he enters into an extended conversation with Abraham in which Abraham pushes the limits of propriety: "Will you save the city if there are fifty righteous in it?"

"Yes."

"Forty-five?"

"Yes."

"Forty?"

"Yes."

Think of it—God allowing Abraham to talk with him this way . . . all the way down to ten.

The unmistakable point here is that the Judge of all the earth will do right with the people he has created. When his judgments fall, there is nothing arbitrary about them. They are a response to human wickedness, and if this wickedness is mitigated by the slightest goodness, he will withhold his hand of judgment.

With all our searching questions, we do well to take the record of this conversation very seriously. On the one hand, it reminds us that there is a direct connection between human disobedience and judgment. We cannot sin against God with impunity. On the other hand, we may be assured that God will save those who are righteous.

And who are the righteous? Those who are covered by the blood of Christ, whose righteousness has become their possession. God, the Judge of all the earth, is totally, entirely, completely fair, and he is so loving that he provides the way of escape from his judgment through Christ's blood.

Judge of all the earth, we praise you because of the revelation of your never-failing right action as you deal with us. Thank you, dear God, for making righteousness a possibility for us, not only through Christ's death but also through the presence of your Holy Spirit in our hearts. Save us this day anew and accompany us in your grace, we pray. In Christ, Amen.

God and the Lowly

Sorry for Sin or fault

"I live . . . with him who is *contrite* and lowly in spirit. . . ."

Isaiah 57:15 *Penitent*

Humble

Few books exalt the holiness of God more than the prophecy of Isaiah does. The prophet began his ministry smitten by God's glory, and early in his book he recorded the angels' call: "Holy, holy, holy is the LORD Almighty; the whole earth is full of his glory" (Isa. 6:3). In the chapters that precede Isaiah 57, the prophet announces God's judgment on Israel and on the nations that surround it.

In the passage we are now examining, however, the prophet announces a marvel that causes us to recoil in amazement. Isaiah provides us with a revelation of God's willingness to live with his people. The theme that dominates the book—that God is exalted and holy—is found in Isaiah 57 along with the announcement that God, in spite of his own splendor, lives with those who are contrite and lowly.

The great deformations of biblical religion are caused by a widespread failure to notice carefully what the Bible is saying here. The statement is simple, and there is nothing confusing about the language. "This is what the high and lofty One says—he who lives forever, whose name is holy: 'I live in a high and holy place, but also with him who is contrite and lowly in spirit, to revive the spirit of the lowly and to revive the heart of the contrite'" (57:15).

If there are Bibles that highlight the words of Christ with red letters, these words, a direct quote from the Almighty, should appear in flaming fire. We must look at them long and think on them carefully. Here God tells us whom he will live with. And is it not true that these words also tell us, consequently, whom he will not live with?

We learn here that we must be contrite and lowly in order to enjoy the presence of God in our lives. And these are not two separate conditions. In Hebrew the word for *contrite* and the word for *lowly* are synonyms. Both of them are heavy with overtones of brokenness, of being crushed, of being brought down from a lofty position to an inferior place. What we are looking at here is humility. God, who dwells in a high and holy place, also lives with the humble. There is nothing more important for Christians than humility, and there is nothing more catastrophic than pride, because pride makes it impossible for God to live with them.

We must notice too that the humility needed for the presence of God is a humility of *spirit*. We are not talking about external life conditions that can be arranged to make it appear as if we are humble; we are not talking about things we can do that will cause others to ascribe humility to us. God is talking with us here about our interior lives.

Because a contrite and lowly spirit is so important, God makes sure that his people experience it. He has given us much to humble us. First, there is his magnificent and seemingly infinite creation. Second, there's the majesty of the holy way of life expressed in God's law. Third, we have received the costliest gift in his holy Son as a sacrifice for our salvation. We look at all this and we put our hands to our mouths; we are speechless—what a gloriously holy and absolutely powerful God we have!

That's true enough, but often we are blind, often we are too busy to notice, and—let's be honest—often we are just too proud: we are "uncontrite" and "unlowly." So God works with each of his people—the good shepherd carefully works with each sheep. He guides our steps and arranges each event in our lives so that there finally comes a time when we lie broken before him.

Sometimes this does not happen in our lives until there has been a gracious intrusion of some kind. Life-threatening illness, a horrible accident, disgrace, failure. Whatever it takes for each of us, God will make sure it happens. And when it happens, we discover the fullness of his presence. God creates "praise on the lips of the mourners in Israel."

Exalted and holy God, we scarcely dare pray because we must confess that we are full of pride. Open our eyes to the splendor of your creation, the wonder of your law, and the perfection of salvation in Christ, and humble us, we pray. Do whatever is necessary to give us contrite and lowly spirits. And please live with us, for Jesus' sake, Amen.

Meditation 38

Follow That Box

"You have never been this way before."
Joshua 3:4

It's scary to embark on something brand-new, especially when the bridges are in flames behind you and there will be no return. The nation of Israel was at one of those points of embarkation, and for them nothing would be the same again. God's promises assured them that they were heading for the promised land, but they knew they would have to fight many battles before they experienced peace and rest in the land.

So the orders came down to each tribe and clan from General Joshua, the son of Nun, of the tribe of Ephraim. Joshua had been Moses' aide for many years; now he was Moses' successor. His message was simple. When the covenant box moves—the ark of the covenant—move out and follow it, and then you will know which way to go. Follow that box "since you have never been this way before."

Oh, the holy box! It was full of the Word of God. In it there lay the tablets Moses had prepared, upon which God wrote his perfect law with his own finger. Israel, what other nation has a God as close as your God is close to you? What other nation has heard his voice and received God's message as you have? And the ark of the covenant represented God's presence. Follow the box with the law in it, O Israel, and you will find your way in the unknown.

There's something here for us who are often called to go somewhere we have never gone before. We prefer to live in familiar surroundings and to do things we have done repeatedly. We like our lives to be fairly settled, with not too many surprises, but there are times when we have to break away into something totally new. Such times often bring high anxiety. The people of Israel must have felt anxious as they saw a new land full of enemies in the distance, across the Jordan at flood stage, making the usually dry land along its banks spongy and treacherous.

The times of transition and change in our lives are small compared to the vast movement of thousands of people described in Joshua 3, but for us they can be as momentous and troubling. Leaving one state or province for another in search of work when you've been caught in a downsizing avalanche is like that. Going for treatment at a cancer center is like that. Leaving a home you have lived in for years and moving into an apartment or a condo is like that. And, of course, leaving this world and crossing your own Jordan over into the promised land is like that.

When we leave the familiar to walk a path we have never traveled before, we have lots of crises. We don't really know who we are. We wonder if we will be able to make it in our new surroundings. Or we doubt whether the promised land will be as good as God says it is going to be. When you travel a road you have never traveled before, you feel lost and forlorn and afraid.

But all this can be good for us because, just when the props of our lives are kicked aside and our self-confidence gives way to anxiety, we can attach ourselves to God in a new and vital way. We must admit it: when the river of our lives runs between familiar banks, we do not always feel our intense need for God. When, suddenly, we face new and unexpected events, we reach up and say, "Precious Lord, take my hand, lead me on, help me stand. . . ."

For Joshua's people, the ark of the covenant led the way into the unknown. We have so much more. In place of God's covenant word on the law tablets, we may follow Jesus, God's dear Son. We live in a time when God's abiding presence has been realized through Christ. We now have God's Word in the Holy Bible. And believers in Christ have the Holy Spirit of God within them.

Yes, in place of Joshua himself, we have Jesus, the "Jeshua" of this age. He is our captain. So those who believe in Christ live each day with confidence, and when the time comes to strike out along new paths and go to new places, even to cross the Jordan into the promised land, we follow our Savior. He will make every day a grace-filled adventure.

Precious Lord, please take our hand as we enter the newness of this hour, of this day. Open our eyes to see that in a very real sense we do not know what the next moment will bring when the phone rings or when the letter is opened. Thank you for always going ahead of your people. Turn our eyes on Jesus, who will surely make this day splendid. In his name, Amen.

His Self-Existence

"I am. . . ."
John 8:24

Jesus and the Pharisees carried on a running battle of words and ideas. The Pharisees could be vicious, and Jesus attacked them with vehemence. John 8 contains one of their most vitriolic conversations. When we read it, we shudder because in it Jesus describes the Pharisees as sons of Satan and talks about the dreadful possibility of dying in your sins.

"If you do not believe that I am the one I claim to be, you will indeed die in your sins" (John 8:24). That's putting the issue bluntly. This statement makes us realize that we had better pay close attention if we want to escape such a horrible fate.

What's fascinating about Jesus' statement, however, is that a part of it isn't really in the Bible at all. If you look at the original Greek text in this case, you discover that Jesus actually says here, "If you do not believe that I am, you will indeed die in your sins." The phrase "the one I claim to be" is not in the original text. (Nor is the word "he" as found in the King James Version, which conveys the idea that Jesus says, "I am he. . . .")

The man who brought this to my attention died a long time ago, but we can still learn from him. William Romaine was an English preacher who died in 1771 just before the American Revolution. As I was going through some old things, I noticed his sermon on John 8:24, bound in a little pamphlet titled "The Self-Existence of Jesus Christ," as it fell to the floor. I was just about to discard it when on second thought I figured I should at least take a look at something with such a serious title. I read thirty-four small pages, tightly packed with solid meat that, among other things, pointed out to me what John 8:24 actually said.

It's understandable that English translations of this passage have added something to the words *I am,* because the entire passage here is about who Jesus is. And in English we are inclined to add something to a clause such as "I am" in order to round out the meaning. But we must forget that, says the old English cleric to us across the centuries. What Jesus is saying here is that he is the God who exists in and of himself. What we have here is Jesus saying he is the very God who appeared to Moses in the burning bush. Remember that. "Just tell them," God said to Moses, "that I AM has sent you."

According to William Romaine, what John 8:24 is saying is that unless a person believes that Jesus Christ is truly God, who possesses his existence in and of himself, that person will die in his sins. Now that's pretty serious talk. And I for one am thankful that Romaine pointed this out. In the Greek text of John 8:24 there's also a margin note referring to Exodus 3:14. There is every reason to believe that Jesus here is referring to the burning bush and is establishing a connection of identity between himself talking to the Pharisees and the Lord God talking to Moses.

The point of this passage, then, is that people will die in their sins unless they understand who Jesus really is. This is a message that needs repeating nowadays when so many people assume that every spiritual road leads straight to glory. That is simply not true. You and I must understand clearly who Jesus is. He is God. Our existence comes from God. His existence as God comes from no other origin than himself. He is the divine I AM in human flesh.

Those who do not believe this, according to Jesus, will die in their sins. To be "in one's sins" is a most dreadful state. Those who die this way take every sin they ever committed along with them to the grave, and when they stand before the judgment seat their every sin condemns them to hell.

Christian believers are those who know that the "self-existent" God has come to live among us in the second person of the Trinity. It is this gloriously divine personage who has given himself for our salvation. That the one and only God has done this is what makes Christianity so marvelous.

Lord Jesus, we worship you. How glorious you are! Strengthen our faith in your holy divinity and encourage us to flee to you alone for our salvation. Our sins are many, but you, O glorious God, have made the sacrifice needed for their removal. We are grateful that you have made it possible for us to die free from our sins and not in them. In your name, Amen.

Meditation 40

His Benefits

Forget not all his benefits. . . .

Psalm 103:2

The human memory is a remarkable phenomenon. Sometimes older people are startled when something that happened ages ago comes to mind from across the years so clearly that it seems it happened only moments ago. How can that be? How can it be that I can recall certain things my father said to me in 1942 just as clearly as if he said them yesterday?

On the other hand, our "forgetteries" are remarkable as well. Who knows why some events seem to have been tossed into a shredder while others can emerge after fifty years just as sharp as a digital photo? Sometimes people tell me, with a straight face, that they clearly remember something I did many years ago, and yet I have not the slightest memory of it. If it is something complimentary, I feign remembrance, and if it is of little consequence, I do not protest. But, of course, if it is something that I feel darkens my reputation, I deny ever having been involved. But later, as I think of my alleged complicity, I marvel that something several people attest to has vanished without a trace from my poor mind.

We should be more careful about remembering; there are times when we should sit ourselves down and harshly tell ourselves that we should not forget something that is extremely important. Such is the picture that comes to mind when we read the poem we call Psalm 103 in the Bible. This poem is a call to praise—not addressed to multitudes, but a call of the self to the self—and the urgent message is *O my soul, do not forget the benefits of the Lord.*

This tender poem provides a catalog of our God-given benefits, and the one that stands far above the rest is God's provision for forgiveness of sin. It's easy to thrust this benefit into the background of our thinking because we often feel we don't need it quite as much as God knows we need it. It can be difficult to remember the benefit of forgiveness because we tend to feel that we do God a splendid service simply by paying a bit of attention to him. When we go to church, we feel that we have chosen some excellent company. It is easy to forget, while songs are being sung, and later, when we kick back and listen to the preacher, that we are Esau-people by nature, closer to Judas than to Paul.

This remembrance of divine forgiveness assures us that God has "removed our transgressions" from us "as far as the east is from the west" (103:12)— and that is good, except that I often succeed in removing them an equal distance from my mind all by myself. To be sure, I do not frequent casinos, I abhor the state lottery, and I have never darkened the door of a bordello, but I do have heart trouble that is quite severe. There are thoughts there that are entirely unworthy of a follower of Christ; as soon as they intrude and I recognize them for the perversity they are, I too am able to remove them from my consciousness as far as the east is west.

"O my soul . . . forget not all his benefits"—and uppermost among them is the benefit of deliverance from sin's wages, which is eternal death.

Psalm 103 also reminds me of God's provision for healing. It's easy to forget this benefit too, especially when one has just received a clean bill of health from the doctor. But God is the one who maintains this fragile and complicated system I call my body. And when things go dreadfully wrong, as they do occasionally, it is God who provides the help. Every heartbeat, every breath, every proper function of organs deep within and out of sight occurs because of God's sovereign control.

We make our daily journey through life encased in the care of Almighty God; he holds us tenderly in his hand. *O my soul, don't forget this.* But there are days on end when I live without giving God's provisions a single thought. How can I forget all this? His forgiving grace? His daily loving care? How?

It's not difficult at all. It's the way we human beings are. We prefer to forget his benefits and think we are getting along just fine.

Lord, we could not be more mistaken. Remove your care for an instant from our lives, and that would be the end of us. And, Lord Jesus, our sins are so great, including the sin of thinking we are not very sinful. Humble us and apply to our broken lives the cleansing of your blood. Holy Spirit, work in our hearts so that we will not forget your benefits. In Jesus' name, Amen.

Meditation 41

Growing and Growing

Grow in the grace and knowledge of our Lord and Savior Jesus Christ. . . .
2 Peter 3:18

In a few more weeks he would be going to kindergarten, and he was starting to think about it a lot. A year or so ago, when we talked about it, the biggest problem was how he would get home each day. He had pretty much worked through that. Now he was thinking about the learning involved. I was surprised to see him sitting on a step in my home, earnestly "reading" a book.

"Are you reading that?" I actually wondered if he might be because the book looked fairly simple. He responded with a serious "Yes."

I looked at the book closely; he seemed to sense my puzzlement and explained, "Tomorrow we are going to a reading club at the library, and I am trying to learn to read by tomorrow."

"Oh, I see," I replied, as serious as he was. I wanted to laugh but this was not something to laugh about, and I wanted to honor his dedication. Later, when a few of us older children got together, I told them about our little conversation, and we laughed heartily. The very idea: a little preschooler trying to learn to read in one day. How cute! And how absurd!

You cannot learn to read overnight. And you cannot become a sanctified Christian overnight. When the angels see how confused we often are about spiritual things, they must feel like laughing too. In fact, they must have a difficult time trying to keep from breaking into gales of laughter, but of course if they did that they'd probably blow their cover.

The apostle Peter closes his brief second letter to the dispersed and persecuted church with a call to "grow in the grace and knowledge of our Lord and Savior Jesus Christ." We can assume that he knew much about the way Christians grow up and mature. It takes time.

The idea behind this is a simple one we are all familiar with. Think of a plant you might notice one hot summer day and how, after just a couple of weeks while you've been on vacation, it has grown twice as large. Being a Christian involves a similar sort of process. A believer may never stagnate or plateau. Believers keep on growing throughout their lives.

We are to grow in the grace and knowledge of Christ. What are these things? In this context grace refers to the gradual development of the gifts of the Spirit in our lives. Thankfully there are cases in which people seem to be transformed nearly instantaneously by the Spirit's power—at the time of their conversion. They may suddenly become numb to the temptations that formerly battered them. But even in such cases, growth follows. Faith, goodness, godliness, kindness—the kinds of virtues Peter mentions in the first chapter of his second letter surely come into the picture. Also involved is the development of the practice and attitude of prayer.

And these virtues grow as we grow in knowledge. For believers today, this means learning more about the wonderful Bible, studying it, meditating on it, discovering the splendor of our salvation, and learning to see our days' and life's circumstances in terms of the Bible's teaching.

In these devotions, we are trying to do that—to ponder God's wonderful ways and to grow in the knowledge of God, our Savior. Part of our growth is the realization that we are often like that little boy who was trying to learn how to read overnight. Sometimes we believers sound just like him. If someone asks us when we became a Christian, we might say, "Five years ago in September, and I remember the day and the hour." Praise God for that. But maybe we should also point out, "I am *growing* more and more as a Christian all of the time. It's a process—and a marvelous one at that. I grow daily."

Sometimes believers are shocked to discover, let's say, at a time of sudden bereavement that when they turn to God for solace, he seems to be far away. Could this be because they have never realized that believing in Christ involves growing? If we are growing in grace and knowledge, we will have the courage to endure when suffering comes, and we will discover that life's harshest moments seem to accelerate our growth.

Lord and Savior Jesus Christ, we are so sorry that we often fail to realize we must grow. It must make you very distressed to see us trying to live as Christians without applying ourselves to spiritual development. The angels likely marvel at our stupidity. Please use what we have thought about today as a reminder to attend to your Word each day. In your name, Amen.

Dead Children

"This brother of yours was dead and is alive again. . . ."
Luke 15:32

The parable of the prodigal son tells us what was in Jesus' mind, and it shows us that he really understands our families. I mentioned that earlier in this book. The parable shows us that when Jesus looks at our families, he sees many dead children.

Parents whose children treat them shamefully and live dissolute lives, going far away so that the parents don't know where they are—such parents should realize that their children have died. It is heartbreaking to bury one of your own dear children, but it is also heartbreaking when a child pursues a wretched, destructive lifestyle of disobedience to God. A child who rebels against God is as dead as a child you bury in the ground. But these dead children can be raised to new life.

From out of Jesus' mind comes a description of the prodigal's behavior in precise detail. The Savior is no ascetic who would be shocked to stumble into the corner bar and hear the foul language there. He knows all about the steamy sex of the clubs. He tells the story straight: the boy began to live like a pig, and he ended up living with pigs. And as the story concludes, Jesus has the father explain to the elder son exactly why a family member can plunge into such degradation: *he was dead.*

Some teenage children who grow up in God-fearing homes die like this, and sometimes they stay dead for many years. Three older couples who had known each other three decades ago had a reunion. As they talked about their children, they discovered that all of them had dead children, no longer teenagers, out there living in bold rebellion against the God they had learned about in their parents' homes. No, these prodigals of theirs no longer lived like pigs; they had become refined and successful, but they were dead nonetheless. So the couples prayed about their prodigal children to Jesus, who understands what is happening even better than they do.

Remember that this story came from Jesus' mind, and that means it came from God's mind. And Jesus wants us to know that children can die in more ways than from being hit by a car. Parents who agonize over their children's behavior must understand the reason why they act as they do. The dead are not capable of living the way their godly parents or their heavenly Father wants them to live. "This brother of yours was dead . . ." said the father in the parable.

But Jesus also saw hope for these dead children. After describing the unworthy son's plunge into the abyss of depravity, Jesus talks about something happening to him: "he came to his senses." Actually the original language here says that "he came to himself." The severity of his lot got through to him. God got his attention. In his poverty, he could no longer have any illusions about how great his life was. Finally he looked at himself. He went within himself. And when he did that, he remembered his origin, his home, his father, and his father's house.

Now, remember again that Jesus is telling this story, and he wants us to know that there are two things that can bring dead children back to life. Circumstances can do it. And then, when the circumstances cause them to turn to themselves, they remember their early years and what they learned and how they lived. To be sure, it's the grace of God that makes this happen, but this is how grace often works itself out in actual life.

Jesus is a realist. Believing parents often are not. They like to think that their children will develop in a straight line from cradle to conversion to a life of faith. If only that were true in every case! No, says Jesus, some children go through a time of spiritual death. But parents should never lose hope. They train up their children in the way they should go, and they never stop praying for them.

No joy surpasses the joy parents feel when a child who was dead is raised to life through the power of God. When that happens, they want to party. Of course they do! While they wait for their children to be raised from the dead, they have lots of reasons to have high hopes.

Father God, we pray today for the children who have strayed away from faith-filled homes. Look on their parents' broken hearts and give them your comfort, we pray. Help us to see the straying children of your covenant people with Jesus' eyes. Please do whatever is necessary for these children to be restored. Thank you for the story Jesus told. Our hope is in him and in his powerful grace. In his name, Amen.

Sine Qua Non

"Apart from me you can do nothing."
John 15:5

"Without which nothing"—that's what *sine qua non* means. It's fancy Latin for something that's essential, such as gasoline for your car. Without gas, the car won't run. Gas is the *sine qua non*. You've got to have it.

Well, Jesus made it about as plain as he could: If we don't have Jesus, we won't be able to do anything. Actually the thrust of the original here is that without Jesus we won't be able to do nothing—it's a double negative that compounds the negative. Without Jesus, negative upon negative.

But what does this mean? There are lots of people who are successful but who don't know Jesus. Their families flourish. Some of them are business-people who are making a mint. Some of them do lots of good things in the community. And think of all the things we do without Jesus, without calling on him—we just do it, and some of it turns out all right.

Well, notice what Jesus is talking about here: "You did not choose me, but I chose you and appointed you to go and bear fruit—fruit that will last" (John 15:16). What we have here is Jesus speaking about human life as it looks when you see it through God's eyes. When God looks at the things we do from day to day—the things we do without Christ, he sees that what we are doing is futile. It's all going to be swept away. But when we live for Christ and with Christ and in his power, our lives are elevated to new levels of performance. What we do in the power of Christ will last forever.

How should we react to the reminder that Jesus is the *sine qua non* of doing anything lasting and worthwhile?

Well, first of all, we should hang our heads in shame. How often have we not tried to do things in our own strength? This is especially true of those who have special natural gifts. Maybe they can sing well; maybe they have the "gift of gab," as we sometimes say. Maybe they are fantastic with numbers and can always make a buck in business because of it. Maybe they are good salespeople. Maybe they figure they can handle their kids because they know some psychology. Whatever. We try so hard, we try to develop our skills, we want to be able to do it on our own. Jesus' words come into our lives, and they cut us down. *O, Lord, please forgive me for trying to be so self-sufficient. I so easily forget my dependence on you.*

But after the shame there should be another feeling that rushes in and drives the shame away. Jesus is the *sine qua non,* but, thanks be to God, he has come here and died for our sins, risen from the dead, ascended into heaven, and sent his Holy Spirit into our lives so that we could become like him. True, we may try to live on our own, but once we have faith in him, we don't have to live on our own.

Jesus did not tell us we can do nothing apart from him in order to taunt us. He told us this in order to motivate us to flee to him. We may abide in him. We can abide in him. We can remain in his love. We can love Jesus, and he will love us. We can ask the Father for all sorts of things in Jesus' name, and his Father will answer us. Oh, we cannot do these things in our own strength, but the very same Jesus who encourages us to abide in him provides his own Spirit so that we can.

How practical the Christian religion is! Think of this day. Think of the work that must be done. Think of the people who must be talked to. Think of those whom you can influence. Think of all the relationships in this day once again, some of them frustrating and baffling. Perhaps children whom we cannot understand . . . or parents. Whatever. But Jesus is reminding us that he is the one who will help us. We had better not try to live out the day on our own. We should turn to him and discover the wonder of what it's like to abide in his love, to be a branch of Jesus himself, who is the vine. Begin the day like this, and expect great things.

Lord Jesus, you are the vine. Make us part of yourself—branches that draw their vitality directly from you. Forgive us for being so cocky and independent. Oh, you know us so well. Receive our confession of sin. In place of our own strength, please give us yours and help us to bear fruit that will last. Thank you. In your name, Amen.

Clothed with Kindness

Clothe yourselves with . . . kindness. . . .
Colossians 3:12

"Clothes make the man." Who said that? Laertes in Shakespeare's *Hamlet.* So? It's true—clothes do have something to do with what we are. Not the latest fashions on an anorectic model walking down the runway with a vacant stare and cocaine chic, of course. But the clothes you wear tend to say something about you.

Colossians 3 uses the idea of clothing to convey what believers in Christ should be thinking as they make their way down the runway of each day. The apostle Paul liked this figure of speech; in Romans 13:14 he tells people with dirty minds to come off it and "clothe themselves with Christ." And in Colossians 3 he identifies several articles of "clothing" Christians should wear to work, to play, and to bed.

Kindness is one of them. Just simple kindness. If there were more of the milk of human kindness, our world would be transformed. Sometimes we Christians can get mad as hob and rant and rage just as furiously as anyone. Sometimes we walk our circle around a person with a disability just as deliberately as anyone. Sometimes we can treat the people we live with every day like dirt. Just when they need us, we can be so wrapped up in our own concerns that we overlook their need for kindness.

How long has it been since you have heard a preacher deliver a sermon on the subject of kindness? I know of no extended discussion of this virtue in theology. Do a search on the Internet for the word *kindness* and you won't come up with much. Read a book about the powerful secrets of the most effective people and you won't find much talk about kindness—although Max De Pree touches on it in his *Leadership Is an Art.*

If a person is genuinely kind, there's a good chance that others will think the person to be rather weak. And, of course, there are some people who are genuinely kind and who don't care if others think they are weak, but a good many of us fall down in this department.

The idea of kindness is extraordinarily important. We know this because kindness is a quality of personhood that is associated with God. In fact, we have been saved by God's kindness. Romans 2:4 speaks of the riches of God's kindness and reminds us that it is God's kindness that leads us to repentance and keeps us from destruction by his judgment. In Titus 3:4 the appearance of Jesus Christ in this world is described this way: "The kindness and love of God appeared. . . ." Think of it!

Oh, kindness is important, all right, and its importance is revealed as well in the fact that you can be clothed in the kindness God wants to see in your life only if you have been re-made by the Holy Spirit. The Holy Spirit is often mentioned in conjunction with the word *kindness*. Kindness is part of the fruit of the Holy Spirit described in Galatians 5.

Kindness is a major player among the Bible's virtues, in spite of how little it excites us. What does it mean in practical, everyday affairs? Well, look at God and us. God's kindness was expressed in response to our need. As long as there is no hurt, no brokenness, no lostness, you don't have to show kindness, but where any of these exist, there should be kindness in response.

One of the best forms that kindness takes is ordinary courtesy, which is showing preference and consideration for other people. Kindness involves a willingness to step aside and make sure that someone else receives what he or she needs.

Here's a litmus test you can use to tell if a person is a growing Christian. Ask if the person is kind. If a person is cruel, selfish, inconsiderate, and unsympathetic, has that person really understood the kindness of God that has been expressed in the sacrificial love that Jesus displayed so dramatically?

Christianity is the most practical religion because it involves transformation. When the Holy Spirit comes into a person's life, that person begins to look more and more like Christ. What happens is that Christians begin to wear Christ's clothes; every day they dress in holy kindness.

Kind and loving God, thank you for letting your kindness appear to us in the coming of Jesus Christ, the Son of your love. Touch our hearts now with the wonder of your kindness toward us and use it once again to bring us to repentance. Give us your Holy Spirit and turn us from our selfishness. Make us sensitive to the needs of others. In Christ, Amen.

Meditation 45

Jealous of Joseph

"If anyone is thirsty, let him come to me. . . ."
John 7:37

The first time I stopped at the hospital to visit Joseph, I was embarrassed that I didn't know his last name. I knew the first few letters of his last name, but I had to ask the receptionist to cite a list of several names that started the same way; then I recognized it when she came to it. I didn't know Joseph before his doctor called me and asked me to visit him. The doctor told me that he had prayed with this very sick patient and that this man had accepted Christ but needed more spiritual attention.

You may have met Joseph a time or two, especially if you spend time on the highway. He may have scared the living daylights out of you when he came up behind you with his big rig. He used to drive for Roadway, sometimes piloting their three-trailer behemoths. "Funny," he said that first day we talked, "when things are going okay in your life, you just never give God a thought." But the day I got his name straight, he was thinking about God.

There are certain special times of high privilege that we ambassadors for Jesus have, and I had such a time that afternoon. It was quite clear to both of us that the disease that began with the removal of one of Joseph's lungs about three years ago had about run its course, and we would not have too many more times to talk about Jesus. He wanted to hear about Christ and about forgiveness of sins and what is going to happen after we die. So that's what we talked about. Just that, after a few initial pleasantries.

As I read some of the marvelous passages from the Bible that cover these subjects, I could hardly keep my eyes on the page. When I glanced at Joseph, his eyes were fixed on me, hardly blinking. It was as if the words of God that spoke of salvation in Christ were the only sound in the world to him, and he was drinking in every one. I am sure Jesus had this man in mind when he said on "the last and greatest day" of the harvest feast, "If anyone is thirsty, let him come to me and drink."

I was jealous of that dear sick trucker as he responded to the good gospel with such total concentration. The gospel is for the thirsty. Water tastes so satisfying when you come in from strenuous exercise on a hot day. So do OJ and Gatorade, depending on how thirsty you are. And the gospel sounds different when its message about forgiveness of sin and a glorious eternal life comes to you when you know you don't have a leg to stand on with God and that this life is going to just drip away one day and be gone like the IV solution hanging by your bed.

When you are in that condition, you pay attention to the gospel. And this is why the church must never stop announcing the gospel everywhere. When you see some truckers tearing off pell-mell down a busy highway, chomping on their cigars, remember that the gospel has to be there for them when the jig is up and they have an oxygen tube up their nose and they start thinking about God and Jesus and hell and heaven. So often God uses sickness to arrest us. He's like a state trooper bearing down on us with lights flashing, spotlight whipping back and forth, siren screaming. "Stop!" he says. "Pay attention to me."

Some of us know the gospel so well—too well. We have heard it often; we have said it often. We have to pray that we too will hear it as Joseph heard it the last days of his life. We have to pray that all the time.

If you come to Jesus and you are not thirsty, you cannot pay attention the way Joseph did—instead you can easily think that you're doing him some kind of a favor. "It's nice of us to come to church, isn't it?" we tend to think to ourselves. "We're willing to take a couple of hours off on a perfectly good Sunday. Nice of us to read our Bibles too, isn't it? And to pray. God must like that."

Yes, I was jealous of that dear man that afternoon. We need to realize every moment we walk this earth that we are poor sinners on our way to hell unless God intervenes. That realization has to be more than theology; it has to be thirst. Jesus invites the thirsty to come to him.

Thank you, gracious God, for intervening in the lives of your people, as you did in Joseph's. Please also intervene in our lives. O Christ, please make our thirst for you and for your blessed salvation insatiable. Remove from our lives anything that keeps us from realizing our desperate need for you, our Savior. In your name, Amen.

Self-Denial Has Nothing to Do with Chocolate

"He must deny himself. . . ."
Mark 8:34

Don't read Mark 8 and other passages that deal with self-denial if you want to keep your life intact. On second thought, go ahead and read them anyway because, if you are like me, you have defenses in place to keep them from changing your life much.

Jesus' teaching about self-denial is actually the central teaching for his followers, but there is no other teaching in the Bible that we are more skilled at side-stepping. It's possible to be very religious and never once come to grips with what Jesus has in mind when he tells us to take up our cross as he has taken up his. I am convinced that I should spend much, much more of my time just meditating on what the self-denial he requires is all about. And I am sure that the more I do that, the more I will discover how much of my life is characterized by self-indulgence—and that's frightening.

When we think of the cross, we often think of the suffering that it represents and that it inflicted on our blessed Savior. But when Jesus talked about it, he apparently saw beyond it to a prior condition of personal commitment to God that made the cross inevitable for him. He would never have experienced the physical and other attendant suffering if he had not decided, before all that, to lay aside the glory that was his eternally in the presence of the heavenly Father. In Philippians 2 the apostle Paul tells us that he emptied himself of all that accompanied his lordship and became the opposite of a lord—a slave. The suffering of the cross followed from that fundamental act of emptying. The Savior who calls us to deny ourselves is the paragon of self-denial; none of our self-denial comes anywhere close to what he did.

The word *deny* in the idea of self-denial means "to put a distance between you and your own self that is so absolute that you no longer live according to your own desires." Peter denied Jesus—that is, he put a separation between himself and Christ to save his own skin. In Luke 12:9 Jesus says that anyone who disowns him before people will be disowned before the angels of God. The Greek word in that passage is from the same root as the one for "deny" in Mark 8:34. It's perilous to overlook what Jesus has in mind here. He is saying, "I did it, and I expect you to do it, and if you don't deny yourself, I'll deny you someday before the angels."

What makes all this so startling for us is that everything in our environment contradicts it. Our society, capitalism (if we want to get economic about this), modern psychology—everything puts the human self in the spotlight. And what makes living in such an environment so much fun is that there are mechanisms inside us that are 100 percent in sync with this emphasis.

It ill behooves me to try to tell anyone what self-denial means for him or for her. I am only saying here what the Bible says. And as I do this, I am so shaken within that I scarcely have any heart to suggest to you what this could mean for you. For me, the question is *What does this mean for me?*

Self-denial has nothing to do with chocolate. True, it may be good, even spiritually salutary, to kick an addiction to Godiva, but that's not self-denial. Self-denial is the denial of my self. The obligation to follow Christ in this way requires that I examine everything I think, say, and do in the light of the question *Who is this for?*

We might see this as a crushing, devastating approach to life, but it's really not. Jesus talks about denying ourselves when he talks about following him. The question is *Do I want to follow him?* And if I do, I have to deny myself, take up the cross of self-denial, and let him rule me.

The little bracelets with the letters WWJD somehow catch what is at stake here: *What Would Jesus Do?* I have to ask myself that question always. And when I look at my life, it seems I have failed him terribly.

Jesus Christ, I hear you, and I am stricken with a sense of deepest failure. O Jesus, often we ask for forgiveness of one sin or another, never realizing that our greatest sin is our failure to make you Lord. Bring us to our senses. Help us to ask always what you want us to do, and please show us what it is and help us to do it. In your name, Amen.

Meditation 47

Crave This Milk

Crave pure spiritual milk.
I Peter 2:2

The old King James Version of the Bible translates 1 Peter 2:2 in terms of "the sincere milk of the word." But if you check out the original Greek text of this passage, you discover that there is no word for *word* in it. The NIV and several other translations keep closer to the original text.

There are good reasons, though, to consider the apostle Peter's call to desire "pure spiritual milk" as a call to take the Bible very seriously. Just prior to this earnest call, Peter notes that Christians are born again "through the living and enduring word of God" (1 Pet. 1:23). Besides, the word for "spiritual" supports the notion that here the word of God is in view.

In a sense, then, what we have here is a serious call to read the Bible with the focus and intensity of a nursing child who wants to be fed. There is much in this figure of speech that can help us think about the reading of the Scriptures that are readily available to us today.

We read different material in different ways. For example, if you're an elderly couple who have invested in a company on which you depend for your monthly income and which is going through hard times, you'll pay close attention as you read an explanatory letter from that company about its losses. You might read it over once or twice carefully and then discuss it. Then you might read it again, wondering what implications this letter may have for your cash flow and livelihood.

One of the major maladies that afflicts long-term Christians is that they grow accustomed to the contents of the Bible. If they attend a church where the preaching of the Word of God is vital, their interest in certain passages will be stimulated by what they hear from the pulpit. But if the preaching in their church is mediocre, possibly not even dedicated to the exposition of the Word, it is very difficult for them to have a voracious appetite for Scripture.

Whatever figure of speech we may wish to use to describe the way we should read the Word of God, the point should be fairly obvious: the Bible can only feed and strengthen us if we read it with a passionate, eager interest.

This can happen only if we realize that this book answers a need that can be supplied nowhere else. Face it, much of the reading we do (if we are among those who still read) is fairly perfunctory. Some of us would not miss a day reading a newspaper, but most of it holds little interest for us. We scan it, read the headlines, and here and there we may find a report we want to read, but even then we will read it fairly quickly and then go on to something else. The newspaper does not answer a deep-felt need.

There are some believers who know that the Bible is a good book and good for them, and they make it a point to read it every day. But they read it as though they are doing a "good work" of some kind that they feel adds something to a sense of merit they accumulate during their brief lives.

When we think of the Bible as spiritual milk and of ourselves as spiritual beings whose spirits are desperately in need of spiritual nourishment, we will spend quality time reading the Bible each day. Peter describes it not only as the book that initiates spiritual life but also as the book that can fine-tune our spiritual lives. The Bible can help us lay aside the natural tendencies that mar our characters and develop a more Christlike demeanor.

Only those who sincerely want to be men and women who truly reflect the virtues of the Lord Jesus will read the Word of God regularly. If we are preoccupied with all sorts of other interests, we will seldom if ever be smitten by the book that is the Holy Spirit's sword.

Those of us who have read the Bible much throughout the years must admit that there are times when it leaves us cold. We must read it diligently and intelligently to minimize such occasions. Most of all, we must go to it realizing that we need it as a nursing child needs its mother's milk.

O Lord, so many hungers and thirsts lead us away from your marvelous Word. Help us to realize our desperate need of spiritual nourishment. Make us sensitive to our own needs as spiritual people who cannot thrive without the special nourishment you provide in Scripture. Feed us, O loving God, with this wonderful milk. In Christ, Amen.

A Thirst Divine

My soul thirsts for you.
Psalm 63:1

Some subjects in the Bible are hard to understand. We North American Christians must confess that we hardly know what they are about. Psalm 63 begins with such a subject: thirst for God. This is a religious experience that eludes most of us.

Several psalms refer to the phenomenon of intense longing for God. The figure of speech expressing this longing in Psalm 42 is well known: we see a deer stricken with deadly thirst and searching frantically for the water it needs. The psalms use language that describes a longing for God that is intense and passionate; it's an excruciating hunger, a ravaging thirst.

This principle in the Bible is extremely unsettling. Those who know church history are aware that some believers had such a burning hunger for God, such an intense devotion that they reportedly bore stigmata, the marks of Jesus' crucifixion. We are mystified as we try to understand what happened in these events.

This principle of longing for God is also unsettling because there is so little of it among garden-variety Western Christians. Could it be that conventional Christianity overlooks the matter of longing for God and dampens that desire when it begins to appear? We talk about "worship wars," battles over what is and what is not appropriate in a worship service, but we talk little about the spiritual longing that should fire our private, personal devotion for God.

For many of us, Christianity is embodied in huge media events and high-profile ministries. We are likely the most highly programmed Christians ever. Because we identify Christianity with the religious exercises that define us as North American Christians, we tend to brush any misgivings aside—we can barely hear the still small voice within us that occasionally suggests there should be more to our Christian experience. Goalsetting and getting things done for God confines our spiritual energy within narrow channels. Our accomplishments provide scant nourishment for our deepest spiritual hunger.

Those of us who view our often frenzied activity with a measure of disdain tend to intellectualize the Christian faith. What is Christianity, we ask? We answer by pointing to our catechism and doctrines; we pride ourselves in sensing nuances of Christian truth, making distinctions and satisfying our curious minds while the part of us that has been designed to have vital communion with God atrophies inside us.

In the light of the Bible's revelation of saints who were sustained by an experience of God's presence, we should be extremely uneasy because of the directions in which the Christianity we know has gone. It is probably true that what we generally consider Christianity is indeed part of the total picture in our lives, but this question persists: If the picture we have exists unaccompanied by a clear longing, a deep hunger and thirst for God, might not the Christianity we know be a defective expression of the faith?

The psalms that express the believer's hunger and thirst for the living God tend, in that context, also to mention God's sanctuary. Psalm 73 is a case in point. The writer, who has been puzzled by the prosperity of the wicked, enters God's sanctuary and sees how rich he is because he has the revelation and comfort of God. "My flesh and my heart may fail," he says, "but God is the strength of my heart and my portion forever" (Ps. 73:26). Today believers themselves have become God's sanctuary in whom the Lord dwells in the person of his Holy Spirit. Because this is true, there must be a fullness of joy in the presence of God for New Testament believers that far surpasses what anyone in the Old Testament era could have experienced.

Now the question is *Do I hunger and thirst for God? Or am I satisfied merely with all the other elements of Christianity?* They are all important, but there is more, much more. And happy are those who want nothing more than communion with the living God. Let them persist in their holy quest. They surely shall be satisfied.

O blessed God, bestow on me the longing, the hunger, and the thirst that many of your saints have had throughout the centuries. Minister to my soul, O God, with your Holy Spirit's presence. "Whom have I in heaven but you? And earth has nothing I desire besides you." Satisfy me with your presence already in this world. In Jesus' name, Amen.

The Book-sized Hearing Aid

The heavens declare the glory of God. . . .

Psalm 19:1

It is inexpressibly sad when you realize that someone you love very much is becoming deaf. When you are thrilled by a quiet and intricate musical score, for example, you look into your loved one's eyes and see no response whatsoever.

These days, when that starts happening, we can get hearing aids that are very effective. They are digital now and computerized so that they do more than just enhance sound. You can drop the little thing down into your ear canal, and it has a plastic string attached so you can pull it out. No one sees it. Pretty neat. People like their hearing aids small, and perhaps that's why a lot of people don't much like the one that's the size of a book.

God wrote a book that helps us hear his speech in nature. Psalm 19 tells us about the way God talks to all of us through what he has created. When you read Psalm 19, you get the impression that the world around us is shouting at us every instant, telling us to think about God and his glory. "The heavens *declare* the glory of God; the skies *proclaim* the work of his hands." The poetry continues, stressing over and over that God's works in nature "declare," "proclaim," "pour forth speech," and "display knowledge." "Their voice goes out into all the earth, their words to the ends of the world" (19:1-4).

It's as if God is shouting at us. Psalm 19 is pretty primitive because in it all this excitement is generated by the plain old sun that rises every morning. The writer here looks at the sun and sees the handiwork of God. Just seeing the sun gets him praising God. If people became that excited then, they should be a million times more excited now.

Now we know that the sun is just one star among trillions of stars. We now know that the earth is a medium-sized planet in one of perhaps millions of galaxies. We have fiddled around a little in outer space, but what we are finding out is telling us how small we are and how incomprehensibly great God is. And now, besides outer space, we have inner space. We know something about the genetic code, about DNA. And where did that come from? It came from God. The same God who made the heavens made our incredibly complex bodies. *Hallelujah!*

Yes, the speech of God is everywhere. But how many of us are saying *hallelujah* today? God is shouting, but nobody is hearing. You look into their eyes, and you see they are deaf. They are drowning in a sea of self-made ignorance that goes by the names of pluralism and postmodernism. The one thing so many say they're sure of is that the God who made everything didn't make anything. That's how deaf they are.

Psalm 19, which tells us how God shouts at us in creation, tells us that in addition to giving us the message written in the sun's daily trajectory, God has also given us a written message. In this poem it's called "the law of the LORD." The Torah—the statutes and precept—had come from Moses. Moses' books told God's people about God and about his creation and about how to live. The Torah was a divinely given hearing aid that enabled people three thousand years ago to hear God when he spoke to them in their own language.

Today, the written revelation of God has been expanded wonderfully. Not only does it contain more pages than it did when this poem was written, but it contains the revelation of Jesus Christ, the Son of God. The Word of God, the Bible, this marvelous hearing aid, tells us this about Christ: "Through him all things were made; without him nothing was made that has been made" (John 1:3).

Without this hearing aid, all of us are deaf to the plain speech of God that resounds through the universe and echoes in every heartbeat. Jesus and the book that tells about him and creation help us to hear. As we believe in Christ and we learn from the book about him, we feel like screaming our response of praise toward heaven. We are overjoyed because we know the God who made all this. We can hear!

Hallelujah!

Creator God, wrap your Word around our lives, drive it deeply into our hearts, and give us our hearing back. So often we are deaf, totally oblivious to the message you send us incessantly from the sun, the stars, the earth, and our own mysterious bodies. Holy Spirit, help us to worship Jesus as our beautiful Savior, the King of Creation. In his name, Amen.

Author and Perfecter

Let us fix our eyes on Jesus. . . .
Hebrews 12:2

We do not naturally fix our eyes on Jesus. There are so many distractions. And focusing on Jesus each day, each hour, somehow seems a bit much. Most people figure that if they pay Jesus some attention on Sundays and special religious holidays, that's quite enough.

Of course, some people don't care to pay Jesus any attention at all because they do not consider themselves to be religious. Others, who actually consider themselves quite religious, don't pay him much attention because of the notion that Jesus is just one religious figure among many. Why should they fix their eyes on Jesus when there are so many other interesting spiritual luminaries?

The only people who can do what we are commanded to do in Hebrews 12:2 are those who are empowered by the very Jesus they are told to look at. There's a circle here. The focus that Scripture is calling for here is an attention to Christ that occurs only when he works in our hearts and cuts through all that distracts us from attending to the most important person who has ever lived. He is, we are told here, "the author . . . of our faith"; he originates it. This is the circle: you can only look at Jesus when he takes command of your eyes.

This reminds those who are familiar with the Bible of passages that speak of faith-filled people receiving the blessings of eternal life *in Christ,* having been predestined in him (Eph. 1:4-5). The Bible does not allow us to believe that interest in Christ rises spontaneously in human hearts. To be sure, all normal human beings observe the universe and sense there is a divine Creator. But this awareness is not the faith that makes us so interested in Jesus that we develop an eye-fixation on him. Such fixation-faith comes from Christ; he takes the initiative.

What's more, the person on whom we are told to fix our eyes is also the "perfecter of our faith." The Bible tells us that Christ, who is the origin of our faith, is also the one who sends his Holy Spirit to make this faith increasingly effective. Before he went to the cross, Jesus told his disciples that his Holy Spirit would come and live within them.

It's humbling to remember that the command to fix our eyes on Jesus is addressed to people who cannot do so unless the person they must look upon fixes their eyes. Those who fix their eyes on Christ are saved people; they may live each day with the assurance that their every moment is under the Savior's control. It's wonderfully exciting to live with one's eyes on Christ, but it is impossible to look at him unless he has first looked at us and provided his grace.

Yes, this is humbling, but it is also wondrously encouraging. For the Bible does not command us to do anything that God does not empower us to do. The same Holy Spirit who inspired these words enters the hearts of those who have been predestined to eternal life and gives them whatever they need in order to look at Jesus. As we ponder this blessed command, we also marvel at the grace that makes it possible for us to obey, and we need not trouble our minds trying to understand just how it all begins and how it works.

Surely we must think of Jesus more than we do. Surely we must attach ourselves to him more steadfastly through the reading of his sacred Word and through the expression of our prayers. There's so much to learn and know about him. When we look closely at his person and his work, we learn to our astonishment that he was executed on the cruelest of all torture instruments when he took our sin upon himself. He bore it all to free us from sin's crushing debt and to glorify us with him.

Fix your eyes on Jesus—all who do this are lifted high above the usual humdrum of life. For them life can be exciting and filled with awe and thanksgiving. They know they have a Savior, and they know their Savior made the first move into their lives.

O Jesus, please help us fix our eyes on you. You know how easily we direct our limited attention to the temporal and the trivial. Help us this day to think of you always and to conduct ourselves as Christians should. We confess that we cannot give you this focused attention without your Holy Spirit. We pray in your name, Amen.

Meditation 51

Incredible

The message of the cross is foolishness. . . .
I Corinthians 1:18

Believers should not be surprised that there are unbelievers. It's important that even those who believe the gospel, who know they must believe it in order to be saved, realize that they believe facts that are, in fact, unbelievable. They should recognize that the good news of salvation through the death of God on a cross is utterly *incredible.*

We do occasionally use the word *incredible* for events that have actually occurred. For example, we might view an automobile that was flattened by a semi and say it's incredible that the driver of the auto walked away from the crash without a scratch.

Of all such events, the event that was necessary for salvation is the most incredible. So we should not be surprised that people are naturally skeptical when we explain "the message of the cross." When we tell them that the very same God who created all things and controls all things died on that cross, the reaction of any human being who is able to think at all is that it could never have happened.

The apostle Paul, interestingly, reminds the Corinthian believers of just how incredible their faith is. Their fellowship has been riddled by dissension, and Paul is distressed, even angry, about this. Apparently he views the marvel of the cross as the antidote to the party spirit that still shatters unity among believers. But he also sees that the unifying force that holds believers together is also the reality that separates them absolutely from others who consider the cross too much to believe.

And he divides those unbelievers into two groups, pointing out distinctions that still help us see just how preposterous the cross really is. One group considers the cross incredible because it contaminates God. The Jewish faith characteristically reacted to the message of the cross by referring to the Old Testament declaration that anyone who hangs on a tree is cursed.

Others view the death of God on a cross as incredible because it reduces to abject lowliness what, by definition, is absolute power and glory. The Greek notion of divinity could never include an idea so ridiculous.

Those who have a dilettante interest in religion can never commit to Christianity—they are forced by their attitude to pursue their fruitless investigations; they talk about religion as myth, and they experience shallow awe as they examine religious curiosities. They may even claim to tap into a cosmic energy source, not realizing that if they have, they have stumbled upon the demonic.

The message of the cross, says the apostle, can only be foolishness to all except those who have been equipped to respond to it by the Holy Spirit. The irony of human religiosity is that it describes the only possible way of salvation as nonsense while it is endlessly fascinated by products of human creativity—and this creativity, which is most active in religion, is truly foolishness.

So the cross must forever remain an incredible foolishness for those who insist on standing above all religious phenomena and making their sophisticated judgments. That God, whom they may call "the ground of being," or "ultimate reality," would endure the ultimate humiliation and powerlessness of the cross is too foolish for them to accept.

And so it is. We who do believe must acknowledge that so long as we view the cross of Christ with human vision, no other description but *Incredible!* applies. But, thanks be to God, the ultimate incredible event has occurred! God, in the person of his precious, one and only Son—the second person of the holy Trinity—was nailed to a cross of wood where he took our sin upon himself and paid the price for all of it. This is so incredible that it can be believed only when the same God who died captures us with his Holy Spirit and creates faith within us.

Holy Spirit of the living God, please don't let our faith waver as we contemplate what happened when Christ died. And please cause the good news of salvation through the cross to be proclaimed so that your people may hear and believe. Jesus Christ, thank you for being crucified for our sins. We praise you Father, Son, and Holy Spirit, Amen.

Meditation 52

Contentment

Godliness with contentment is great gain.

I Timothy 6:6

Some people, as you may know, have pointed out that Calvinism is responsible for the economic system we call capitalism. It's interesting, though, that when Russia cracked open in the early 1990s, there were businesspeople there who were interested in finding out about John Calvin because they thought he might be able to restore their nation's destitute economic system.

But when we read the Bible (and really understand Calvinism, by the way), we discover that there is much in the Bible that tends to make people view wealth as being of secondary importance—so much so that one is left wondering how a person formed by the Bible could be a success-driven capitalist at all.

When Paul wrote to the young preacher Timothy, among other things he counseled him on how he should deal with rich people and with people who hankered to be rich. He suggested that Timothy remind such people that money-love is the source of all kinds of evil. He told him, further, that discontent—always wanting more—is bad for you. Better to have godliness and contentment.

It's difficult for us to think about contentment for more than thirty seconds or so because so much in our environment gives us the impression that, if we are contented, we are probably sick. Contentment is a pathology. And if anyone has the slightest tendency to fall back into this contemptible state, there are all sorts of stimuli prepared to jerk that person back to reality.

There's something in us that admires Mother Teresa, but there's a lot more in us that admires Bill Gates. Mr. Gates, as you may know, has built a 53-million-dollar house, located along five hundred feet of waterfront, lavishly outfitted and bristling with the latest electronic technology. And to this we resonate.

If contentment, however, is a virtue, Mr. Gates—and we too when we try to be like him—are decidedly unvirtuous. When we read Paul's statement to Timothy, it becomes clear that <u>the state of contentment can be achieved only along the path of godliness.</u> Godly people are contented people. Might the converse also be true?

Paul's simple statement about the intimate relationship between godliness and contentment serves us with a call to examine our lives. Few would deny that contentment is a state of mind, an attitude, that pays rich dividends. Contentment, in addition to the euphoria it provides, is good for our immune systems, and it may even lower our blood pressure and cholesterol.

According to the apostle Paul, this highly desirable state cannot be enjoyed if it is pursued as an end in itself. Contentment is, rather, a by-product, and it's the by-product of a spiritual condition that goes by the name of godliness.

What is godliness? Isn't it just faith? No. It's the blessed result of using the gifts of grace fully. We must, says the apostle Peter, add to our faith goodness, and part of the goodness package is godliness, which he connects to perseverance and knowledge and several other virtues. In the same chapter in which Peter speaks of these things, he announces that God's "divine power has given us everything we need for life and godliness" (2 Pet. 1:3). In other words, the rich ministry of the Holy Spirit of the living Christ results in making believers sufficiently united to God and sufficiently like him to make it possible to describe them as godly people.

What is so sobering about our lack of contentment and lack of godliness is that, if we are honest, we must admit that we often prefer other things in place of God. We do not long for God, we do not pant for him, as the writer of Psalm 42 puts it. The hungers and thirsts we have developed over the years are such that we keep trying to satisfy ourselves with things, with gadgets, with wood and stone and steel. The world has become a flea market, and we have become scavengers.

Lord, we see how miserable we are; we actually want things more than we want you, our God. Minister through your Holy Spirit's regenerating power so that we will be transformed deep within. Lord, we believe in you, but often we fail to use all you provide to make us godly. Make us godly, we pray, and give us contented hearts. For Jesus' sake, Amen.

Meditation 53

Dog Tags

Your young men will see visions. . . .

Acts 2:17

Bracelets, necklaces, earrings—some of us will never understand why young men wear these. Earrings especially. The leaders of some Christian high schools have concluded that earrings have no special meaning really, and if a male student wants to wear them, okay. Some of us say, "Okay . . . maybe." And the necklaces I saw the other day on two stalwart young men, eighteen or twenty, seemed strange on their strong necks, tanned from a summer at the lake. Each of them had two of them, one of which was made of little pieces of macaroni or something like that, all different colors, pink and blue and yellow. These were big guys, sitting in front of me at a worship service at a resort. As I reacted to the necklaces, I began to think about dog tags.

Forty-five years ago, these young men would have been drafted, or they might have enlisted because their buddies were being drafted, and they would have worn a necklace then too, a necklace made of steel, with dog tags attached. If I'd have tapped my young coworshipers on the shoulder and asked if they knew what dog tags were, I probably would have drawn a blank.

Dog tags are made of metal, with the data pressed into the surface; this information cannot be changed. It tells your name, serial number, blood type, and religion—Protestant, Jewish, or whatever. What impressed me about dog tags was the notch in the end of them. Soldiers were informed that the notch was there to help fit the tag between their teeth if they were killed. Their jaws would be clenched together with the notched end of the tag jammed between their teeth and the other end of the tag inside their mouth. That way the soldiers could be identified easily. So around their necks young men used to wear a necklace that told people exactly who they were when they were dead.

The difference between necklaces made of colored beads and dog tags is enormous. No wonder grandfathers often gaze without recognition at their teenage grandchildren. Kids nowadays don't grow up with the thought of being drafted, with the possibility of being wounded or killed. It just doesn't enter their minds. For the older generation, it was the war first, and if you made it through, then you could get on with your life. Circumstances that differ create different kinds of people. Face it, that's the way life is.

But, as I mentioned, we were in church together, worshiping God. And it's there where the bridge can be built between young people and those who are older who have been formed by totally different experiences. Those who wore their dog tags several decades ago and who still remember the anxiety that paralyzed them when they faced combat—those Christians who are now older may realize, in the Spirit-filled place of worship, that the God who saved them, cared for them, and brought them back home years ago is able to use all his children together now to further his great purposes.

And those who are younger, who baffle us sometimes with what seems to us inappropriate dress or behavior, are often in tune with God's Word as much as anyone. Among them are those who have seen the visions the prophet Joel spoke of, the visions Peter preached about when the Spirit was poured out on Pentecost. The vision of these younger people can often lift us all beyond the tired judgmentalism that sometimes afflicts those of the dog-tag generation who are still with us.

The dog taggers must remember that what Joel wrote and what Peter preached about is a statement of what God will surely do. This is the way it is going to be. Young men, who may wear colored beads around their necks, will surely experience the wonder of God's Spirit if they are trusting Jesus.

Those who worship God in spirit and in truth are a fascinating multitude. They are not an army in the sense that they dress the same and march in lock-step past a reviewing stand . . . and wear dog tags . . . but they are an army because each has been transformed by God's Holy Spirit into a Christian soldier. This is why it's always good to see old dog taggers and guys with necklaces embrace and worship God together.

Holy Spirit of the living God, make it possible for God's people who are from different generations and who have been formed by different circum-stances to appreciate and learn from each other. O God, we are so differ-ent. It is easy for us to feel proud . . . and smug . . . and to be so wrong about each other. Give young men visions, please, and help us all benefit from what they see. In Jesus' name, Amen.

Instead of "Twoness"

"They are no longer two, but one."
Matthew 19:6

A minister who had the habit of making shocking remarks commented to a church janitor one evening about a wedding rehearsal that was going on in his church: "In two weeks they'll be throwing things at each other." When the janitor reported this remark to me, I was shocked that a man of the cloth would be so cynical about marriage.

Fortunately the pastor retired years before such remarks would finish off a preacher's career. Those who heard about his comment accepted it as one of his idiosyncracies. Possibly they did not press charges because they realized he could be right.

Couples who are very demonstrative about their affection for each other before their wedding often become mortal enemies afterward. Given the way marriage health affects not only the partners but also their children, the government is now showing an interest in programs that promise some hope of correcting the current divorce epidemic.

Unfortunately there is widespread disagreement about whether government programs help very much. In May 1997 a meeting of marriage and family therapists was shocked when John Gottman, considered the dean of investigators of marriage health and pathology, declared that all his previous research was worthless and that it would take five years and fifty million dollars of government money to do a study that might possibly lead to programs with some promise of alleviating today's widespread marital anguish.

If the pastor I mentioned was a realist about marriage, there is reason to suspect that his cynical comment was not only caused by his experience with parishioners who would drift into his study and unload their marital irritations on him. As a student of the Bible, which he unquestionably was, that pastor also likely found much within the Scriptures that could be used to support his cynicism. The Bible's pages report few instances of outstanding marriages, except perhaps for that of Joseph and Mary, of which we know little. Some observers might suggest that Ananias and Sapphira communicated with each other well and shared common goals (to the bitter end), but citing their example does little to destroy cynicism. The Bible's teachings about marriage must be inferred from several passages. And Jesus' response to the Pharisees who asked him if divorce was ever okay ranks at the very top of those statements that can help us as we think about our marriages and those of others.

For Jesus, the basic reality about marriage is that it makes a couple "one." It moves a woman and a man from separateness, or "twoness," to "oneness." When he responds to the Pharisees, whom we should consider well-meaning in their query, he points out that talking about dissolving a marriage is like talking about removing the fragrance from perfume. You just cannot do that. It's as if he says to them, "Look, guys, you don't know what you are asking. You just don't understand. We have a different name for each—*husband* and *wife*—but, really, the concepts of husband and wife are just two ways of looking at one reality, and that one reality is that they are *one flesh.*"

If we could get that straight in our heads (and hearts), we would be a long way in halting the divorce epidemic. The problem is that you can't have this straight unless you have faith. You have to believe that the Bible's description of the origin of marriage, found in Genesis 2, is accurate. You also have to believe that all the variations on the theme of monogamy in the Bible are aberrations. And you have to believe that Jesus has got it right.

Those who are supported by such faith do not by any means have problem-free marriages, but they know they must work their problems out this side of the divorce court. And they discover that the God who tells them the truth about what marriage really is also equips them to make their marriages beautiful. It's true: they're not two; they're one.

O Lord, you ask us to believe so many things—about you, about our personal selves, and about our union in the holy bonds of marriage. You know how easily we become cynical; you know how quickly our marriages can deteriorate. Please give us a faith that will enable us to have lasting marriages that are as beautiful as they can be. Help us listen to you. In Jesus, Amen.

Chow/Lab

The evil I do not want to do—this I keep on doing.
Romans 7:19

Whenever I visit people for the first time and they have a big dog, I am always wary. So when I visited the people with the walnut farm outside of Lodi, California, I reacted to their dog with suspicion, and it showed. The animal was large and husky and not particularly friendly. The owner apparently noticed how uncomfortable I was and explained the pedigree of the creature.

"It's a cross between a Chow and a Lab," he said. "I was reading a book about dogs, and I learned that the breed least likely to bite a person is a Lab and the breed most likely to bite is a Chow." Then he added, "I think my dog has a hard time figuring out which nature to follow."

When I was four years old, a Chow rose slowly to its feet and planted his teeth in my leg; I can still see it happen in slow motion. So I was relieved when the walnut farmer shooed his dog away. How could anyone be sure whether the dog was having a Chow day or a Lab day?

If being a mixture of Chow and Lab is hard for a dog, being a mixture of two natures, one starting to look more and more like Christ and the other remaining rebellious against God, is hard for believers. We would expect to hear about how hard it is from a newly converted believer who is trying to replace bad habits with good, but we don't really expect to hear how hard it is from seasoned followers of Christ. Well, the apostle who wrote Romans 7:19 was about as seasoned a Christian as there could be, and he complained that his old nature gave him moments of misery every day.

It's almost preposterous to think that this man, Paul, who had been converted by an encounter with the glorified Christ and had likely made a special visit to heaven (2 Cor. 12:1-4) by the time he wrote this, was still severely troubled by his sinful nature. Some scholars have tried to solve this apparent contradiction by asserting that Paul is writing here about his condition before he became Christ's apostle. Good try.

That argument doesn't stand up because there is nothing here that supports the idea that Paul is writing about his past rather than his experience at the time this was written. But mostly it doesn't stand up because those who have been believers for many decades will tell you that they know exactly what this man was talking about. He was talking about the mystery of the actual experience that born-again Christians have: they really do believe; the Holy Spirit is really working in their hearts; they are really beginning to look more and more like Christ—but, doggone it, they have their Chow days, their really bad moments when their old natures erupt, and you wouldn't think they'd even been converted.

Ever "been there, done that"?

Anger can sometimes rise up inside you in a matter of seconds, and you can become furious because your pride has been hurt. (There is anger that is good, but that's not the kind we're talking about.) You can feel this anger grow like a mushroom cloud deep within, and you know that unless you do something quickly you are going to lose control altogether.

Or lust, quirky, demeaning, and captivating, can suddenly take over, and you are embarrassed by yourself. "This shouldn't be happening to me," you say, but it is. "Come on," you say to yourself, "why am I doing this? What's the matter with me?" It takes a lifetime for the powerful forces of our sinful nature to be put in chains, and it's foolish to drop your guard and think you have become as obedient to God as the angels.

All kinds of little pesky sins are also so much a part of us that we have come to accept them as tied up with our nature. Envy, sloth, gluttony, selfishness—all of these and many more. "It's just the way I am," we say. And that is true. This is our nature, our old nature, the residue of perversity that trips us up like a loose shoestring.

O Lord, we are just like the ancient apostle, and now we cry out as he did: "Who will deliver us?" We are thankful that as soon as we ask this question, we know the answer: You will deliver us; Christ will. Forgive us for being so permissive with ourselves, and forgive us for falling again and again. We say it so often, but we must say it again: "O God, be merciful to me, a sinner!" Please. In Jesus' name, Amen.

Meditation 56

God, Our Rock

The LORD is my rock. . . .
Psalm 18:2

"When you are with him, would you please read for him? Please read some of the Bible passages that talk about God as our rock, our shield, the one who will help us. That's what he needs to hear. Everybody tells him he is going to die soon, and he knows that. Even the doctor told him yesterday, 'You're going to die, Joe'—but maybe he won't die right away. Would you please read about God as our rock? Even if he seems to be asleep, he needs to hear that."

Joe's wife wanted me to visit her husband and check on him in the morning because she was apprehensive about the care the hospital was giving him. "Check his feet, please; they have been swollen," she said. "And make sure he's clean." She had to be in court and couldn't do it herself. I promised to take care of all this for her, and I assured her that I would read to Joe from passages in the Bible that would encourage him to fight for his life.

I give her a lot of credit. What was bothering her was that everyone was writing her husband off. He wasn't very old, really, and though she knew his illness was terminal, she needed him for a few more months, even a few more years. And she didn't like the way it seemed as if his doctor and other medical people had buried him already.

Her husband and I had talked together about dying, and he had assured me that his trust for salvation was in God alone. So when we were together the next day, I did what his wife had requested. He was encouraged when he heard the words of Psalm 18, expressed by someone who had been in mortal danger about three thousand years ago: "The LORD is my rock, my fortress and my deliverer; my God is my rock, in whom I take refuge. He is my shield and the horn of my salvation, my stronghold. I call to the LORD, who is worthy of praise, and I am saved from my enemies."

Whatever the circumstances that called those words from the writer's heart, they must have been quite similar to her husband's. The writer talks about the cords of death entangling him and coiling around him. Yes, the coils of death will do that. They will wrap themselves around a person so he cannot move, and everyone nods in agreement: the end is near; the end is near.

But this psalm speaks of deliverance, of a God who reaches down, takes hold of his stricken people, and draws them out of danger. It is so easy to give up. We must not do that. As we sometimes say, "As long as there is life, there is hope." That's always true, but for those who trust in the Lord as their rock, it's true on the deepest level.

Just think, as you look into the faces of your friends and acquaintances, how many of them at one time or another were given up for dead. But they kept on trying, using medical or other means that offered a promise, however slight. They are survivors; they are those whom we never thought would walk again, but they are doing so. We never thought we would see them living normal lives, but they are doing so.

Christians pray to God their rock because they know there are so many good reasons why God might well intervene in hopeless cases and reverse the physician's grim prognosis. Sometimes, if for no other reason, it seems as if God wants the medical profession and all the rest of us to realize that life and restoration come ultimately from God, who is the great physician.

So it is the Lord who is our rock, and this gracious Lord has walked among us in the person of Jesus Christ of Nazareth. He went about healing the sick and in some instances even raising the dead. Roman Catholics have their special saint for hopeless cases; we Protestants have none, but we have God himself, who hears and answers the prayers of his anguished people.

"Just tell my dying husband that," she said. "Pray with him, and read him the wonderful words about God being our rock. I want him to know that, and he will hear you even though he seems to be asleep."

O God, so often we seem to be asleep as we stumble along, beaten down by the catastrophes that make our lives so pathetic. We are jubilant that on this day we may thank you because you have assured us that no matter what our situation is, you are our rock, our refuge, and our shield. O Lord our rock, save us this day. For Jesus' sake, Amen.

We Hate This Word

Humble yourselves . . . under God's mighty hand. . . .
I Peter 5:6

There are many words in the Bible that we enjoy; just saying them gives us good feelings. In some cases there is really no relationship between the meaning of words and the way they make us feel; for example, Mark Twain writes of a woman who said that just hearing the word *Mesopotamia* made her feel good all over. But there are other words—like *gospel, mercy, love,* and *brother* and *sister*—that refer to such good and wholesome things that we may rightly enjoy using them.

There is one word, however, that we hate; that's the word *submission.* (Sometimes the Greek word for this is also translated *subjection.*) Submission is decidedly undemocratic. It suggests that marriages, families, and society as a whole have a specific arrangement in which certain people must obey the decisions of others. Of course, we might not come right out and say we hate this word, but when we examine our heart-reaction to the Bible's message, we have to admit we feel a lot differently about *submission* than about *love,* isn't that right?

The book of 1 Peter brings up the idea of *submission* rather frequently. The apostle Peter was writing to an element of the church that was being sub-jected to irritation and even persecution by the government. Even so, the apostle called the believers to "submit . . . to every authority instituted among men: whether to the king, as the supreme authority, or to governors . . ." (1 Pet. 2:13-14).

Submission is important because it keeps society from disintegrating into chaos; that's why the apostle talks about *submission* in connection with government, marriage, and the home. But *submission* is not only impor-tant because of its practical usefulness. It is also important because it is a basic form of Christian behavior that indicates that a believer understands what the Christian faith is all about.

There is, you see, a prerequisite condition of attitude if we are going to be submissive—we must be humble. Humility is the fundamental heart condition of believers. In 1 Peter 5 we are reminded of this central rule of God's kingdom: "God opposes the proud but gives grace to the humble." The Old Testament prophet Isaiah also marveled at God's willingness to dwell with humble people: "I live in a high and holy place," says the Lord, "but also with him who is contrite and lowly in spirit, to revive the spirit of the lowly and to revive the heart of the contrite" (Isa. 57:15).

Similarly the first readers of Peter's letter were told, "Humble yourselves, therefore, under God's mighty hand, that he may lift you up in due time." Submission, then, is the specific expression of humility required as proof that we understand the gospel and that we truly want to live according to the gospel.

St. Francis of Assisi stands on the pages of history as a person who realized the importance of humility. He lived a life of submission because Christ was his model, and when he examined Christ, he saw the person who had humbled himself even to death on a cross. Jesus is the primary example of total self-denial. Francis wanted to be like him, so he denied himself, striving to be like Christ in his death and in his obedience to his Father in heaven.

Though we hate the word *submission*, we must learn that submitting is an important part of the Christian life. For those who have been overwhelmed by the wonder of Christ's submission to his Father's will and his submission to the Roman government to death on a cross, it is entirely in order to actively seek ways in which they can demonstrate their submission to others. True, it goes against all we are taught these days about self-esteem, assertiveness, and individual human rights. But self-denial is fundamental if we wish to follow Christ, and we must ask for grace to overcome our natural tendency to hate submission so that we may actively seek ways to show our understanding of what it means to follow Jesus.

Lord Jesus, please overpower our natural tendency to be proud and self-assertive. May we take your call to self-denial seriously, taking up our cross again this day. May we respond to the way you have ordered society and the family by willingly expressing submission. You know how we dislike doing this. Conquer us, O Spirit of Christ. Amen.

Meditation 58

153

It was full of large fish, 153. . . .
John 21:11

Long before James Dobson told fathers to pay attention to their sons (in fact, probably before the dear man was even born), my sainted father understood without anyone telling him that his son needed him. So he took me fishing often; one fishing trip to Dunkin Lake, about twenty miles from our home, stands out in my mind.

We fished Dunkin Lake fairly often and seldom had to clean fish afterward. On one occasion we determined to start early in the morning, hoping that that would change our luck. We drove to the lake the evening before and slept in the car that night; my father had done something to the seats in that '33 Ford so that with some twisting it was possible to lie down and sleep. Before dawn we opened the car doors, which opened from the front on that model, and staggered sleepily to the fog-covered lake. We fished for many hours. Our luck did not change. It may have been on that trip that my father sagely commented that it sure was great to be out there fishing, but it was also wonderful that we didn't depend on it for our livelihood.

Perhaps it's experiences like those that always cause me to be startled when I read John 21 and learn the actual number of large fish taken in a miraculous catch: 153. I always feel that this data is there especially for us for whom any number of fish is a marvel. People show me pictures of themselves holding a string of bass—and I suspect the photos have been tampered with. What must it be like to catch a really big fish . . . or to catch twenty at a crack or even more? What a thrill that must be!

Actually, encountering the number 153 in John 21 is an even greater thrill because much can be learned from it. There is no section of divine revelation more rich and profound than chapters 13 through 21 of the gospel of John. When one takes the time to read these chapters together without interruption—and very early in the day—they are truly overwhelming.

In chapter 21 the crucifixion and the resurrection are past, and the magnificent book of John draws to its marvelous conclusion. The apostle Peter is about to be re-instated to full, even leadership, status within the apostolic band, and just before this event John makes sure we know how many fish were caught at the command of the resurrected Lord. This detail confirms our conviction that the inspiration of this holy record extends to every word. And it underscores that the Christian faith is anchored in ordinary realities. Here the carpenter who became the Savior tells the fishermen apostles where to fish. And he had it right.

Surely, the miraculous presence of 153 flipping, flopping large fish brought back memories of another miraculous catch that occurred in much the same way. Luke 5:1-11 tells us how Jesus told Peter and the rest of them to go out into deep water and throw out their nets after they had spent an entire night with as much success as my dad and I had at Dunkin Lake. The catch then was so large that their boats began to sink. Peter was overwhelmed: "Go away from me, Lord; I am a sinful man!" he had cried. Then Jesus announced that these fishermen would continue their trade but that they would catch men instead of fish. "So they pulled their boats up on shore, left everything and followed him."

The 153 fish bring the gospel narrative full circle. If the miraculous catch Luke records caused Peter to call out in confession of sin, he must have been embarrassed at the reminder, during the catch of 153 fish, that Jesus was divine and that he himself was sinful. How often he had wept because of his denial of the Savior. Though he had been present at the post-resurrection events, the memory of his vehement denial must have caused deep uncertainty about his future role as a follower of Christ.

The Bible—what a marvelous book! A book that provides us with information so precise can be trusted for its careful provision of those details that are necessary for salvation. And as we cry out, awestruck and humbled, "We are too sinful to have anything to do with you," Christ receives us into his service once again.

O Holy Spirit, why did you give us the number here? We really didn't need to know. But thank you for doing so because there is much we can learn from your sacred Word to us. We praise you, triune God, for arranging for our salvation and for making sure that from your blessed book we can learn all we need to know to be saved. In Jesus' name, Amen.

Meditation 59

Camels, Read Carefully

"All things are possible with God."
Mark 10:27

Many of us, when confronted by an especially daunting task, will reassure ourselves that we should just rely on God because all things are possible with God. The Bible does in fact make this statement, but we should be careful how we apply it because it refers to a very specific impossibility—that of a rich person being saved. Jesus said that for a rich person to be saved is about as impossible as a camel passing through a needle's eye. Some say Jesus must have smiled when he said that because the figure of speech is so ridiculous.

I doubt he smiled. The subject here is too serious for smiles. We should shudder when we read this because most of us are rich—perhaps not compared to Bill Gates or Sultan Hassanal Bolkiah of Brunei, but certainly compared to a majority of the world's population. And we don't have to be very rich for riches to be like cement shoes on a drowning man.

Fellow camels, what does this mean? Well, Jesus said these words after a rich young man walked sadly away from him. Jesus' disciples had likely been greatly encouraged when the man came up to Jesus because a winner like this was proof that at last the Jesus movement was catching on. They had plenty of common, ordinary riff-raff. This man, on the other hand, had a future and perhaps a position of religious leadership, and he respected Jesus enough to bow before him.

It looked as if the rich young man had everything going for him. He respected Jesus and Jesus loved him; he loved the law of God and kept it; and, by the way, he was rich. Then Jesus said, "What you have to do, my friend, is sell everything you have and give it to the poor and you will have riches in heaven. Then you can come and follow me." Suddenly the expression on the young man's face changed. And he left—bewildered, hurt, frustrated. Jesus' demand was craziness to him. The very thing in his life that proved he had found favor with God—that very thing was what Jesus told him to jettison.

Most of us have tried very hard to squirm from beneath what seems to be the obvious teaching here—that riches are not good for spiritual life and we should get rid of them. Well, Jesus couldn't have meant that—or could he? Certainly he was pointing out here that trusting riches is fatal. If you put your wealth ahead of Christ, you are headed for hell. It's a very simple equation, and every one of us who has what we call *discretionary income* (more than is required for food, shelter, and clothing) should take this passage seriously. The idea of rich people becoming poor because they don't want their riches to get in the way of their relationship with Christ—that's something like a camel going through a needle's eye, isn't it? Yes, there must be something of that in this episode: Don't let your riches come between you and Christ.

I have a feeling, though, that the real reason the rich young ruler didn't want to get rid of his riches was that he believed they were precisely the proof that showed God looked on him with favor. That's the way God's people figured things in those days: if you were rich, that meant you were righteous with God. If you were not righteous, God wouldn't bless you, would he? Analyze all the biblical reports of Jesus' conversation with the rich young ruler, and you get the impression that he came to Jesus with a list of credentials that shouted out to high heaven: Here is a man whom God really loves! Look—he respects Jesus, Jesus loves him, he keeps the law, he wants to know more about being saved, and *he's rich!*

Jesus said to the young man, and he says to us, "The only way you can be saved is through me. Forget your religiosity, forget your dilettante interest in religion, forget your riches, and think only of me." As the apostle Paul said, "I count all these other things as garbage; all I want is the righteousness that comes through faith in Jesus, my Lord" (see Phil. 3:8).

Come to think of it, the apostle Paul in his younger days looked a lot like the young man who came to Jesus. I wonder if that's who he was. Maybe. One thing I know: when I see the way the rich young ruler thought, he could have been me.

All-powerful God, look in your mercy on us camels. Oh, you know how hard it is for us to let go. We love our possessions. We love the power that goes with them. They make us feel so strong and capable and successful. Through your power, O God, please take us through the needle's eye and enable us to depend solely on Jesus' blood for our salvation. For his sake, Amen.

Lot's Wife

"Remember Lot's wife!"
Luke 17:32

Many of us who consider ourselves Christian do not actually do what Jesus tells us to do. To be sure, we do what our circle of Christian people routinely consider Christian actions, but our circle of Christian friends is not the great authority on what Christians should be doing. For example, how often do we remember Lot's wife? I have to admit that I have seldom thought of her. Hardly ever. Even when I read Luke 17 in my general Bible reading, I glide over this command in a heartbeat, and if I think of the woman Lot married for even a moment, my remembrance of her vanishes quickly.

But there it is—a command of Jesus himself, in red letters in some Bibles. We must assume that he was totally serious about this, and what he says is not hard to understand. Jesus is telling us that somehow this woman must figure into our view of things. If we forget her, we are apt to make serious mistakes about the world we live in and about the way we ought to relate to it.

So far as we know, Lot's wife was a native of Sodom, and as Abraham's nephew became more acclimated to Sodom, he met her and married her, and together they raised their two daughters. She apparently had little interest in the true God who had appeared to Abraham; Lot knew something about him because of his association with Abraham. Lot's wife seems to have considered Abraham's God a bother. She didn't communicate much about the true God to her daughters, and certainly not to the young men her daughters were engaged to. The next generation of Lot's family were citizens of Sodom all the way.

Anyway, when God's judgment was about to fall on Sodom and Gomorrah because of their extraordinary wickedness, Lot's wife had to be virtually dragged out of her house, down the street, and out the gate by God's special messengers. They literally had to take her firmly by the hand. Her future sons-in-law wouldn't even budge. So off went Lot and his wife and their two daughters. The divine messengers told them to run as fast as they could, and then they said, very specifically, "Don't look back. Understand? Don't look back." After they had put some distance between themselves and the city, God sent his fire on "the cities of the plain," and that was the end of them. Lot's wife should have got the message, but she didn't. She looked back and in that fatal moment she became a pillar of salt. (See Gen. 19.)

When Jesus told us to remember her, he did not mean that we should have her on our mind all the time, but he asks us to remember her in connection with a powerful teaching in Luke 17. There he tells about the "lightning day"—the day when the Son of Man (Jesus himself) will appear again, illuminating the entire heavens as lightning does on a stormy summer night. Then this earthly order of things is going to be destroyed. It will be as it was when the angel messengers took Lot and his family by the hand and dragged them out of Sodom. As soon as Lot was outside, the firestorm began. But Lot's wife was so attached that she couldn't bear to leave, and she died right there on the spot, possibly so surrounded by the fire, the sulfur, and the fumes that her body changed in an instant to a salt-like statue in the desert.

About the only time I think of Lot's wife is when the flight attendants say with a straight face that in the event of a crash, there will be lights on the floor that will lead me to an exit. "Exit the plane at once," they say, "and don't take any of your hand luggage with you." I wonder about the lights—will they really be there? I doubt it. And if it actually happened, I guess I would try to take my briefcase. And that might be the end of me.

"Remember Lot's wife!" Lord, I will. And my remembrance of this woman reminds me that I must consider the city in which I live—the great city-nation of North America. Is it much like Sodom? Am I so attached to it that I would embrace it while the firestorm raged around me? My eternal destiny has something to do with the answers I give.

Lord Jesus, help me remember that ancient woman who is not so different from me. Teach me to understand that there are many similarities between her world and mine. Lord, break whatever attaches me to this age so that I will flee to you each day. Lord, when the firestorm comes, I want to be able to leave and flee to you. In Jesus, Amen.

The Spirit of Power

God did not give us a spirit of timidity, but a spirit of power, of love and of self-discipline.

2 Timothy 1:7

A major hurdle, if one is going to understand the Bible, is the need to lay aside the notion that it was written for someone else, not for me . . . not for us. One might assume, for example, that the apostle Paul's advice to Timothy is for first-century preachers who are just starting out. But if we restrict this to preachers, that's a pretty narrow subset among human beings. And if we figure that now is totally different from then, Paul's words here won't do us much good.

Preachers, though, are not a race apart; they are merely members of Christ's body who are called to preach and pastor. So it's reasonable to believe that the Holy Spirit arranged to have Paul's statement to Timothy here included in Scripture so that we could apply it to our lives. In other words, we can say, along with Paul, that God has not given us "a spirit of timidity but a spirit of power, of love and of self-discipline."

The timidity that Paul so disdains here is not timidity in general but the natural apprehension that sets in whenever we become vulnerable or begin to look odd because of the Savior. For example, a Christian who has become a high-powered executive who has no fear of anything or anyone may shy away from showing his faith in public. His colleagues may have heard hints that he is a believer, but he may make sure that he gives little evidence to support the charges against him. If so, then this high-powered executive is a very timid person when it comes to standing up for Christ and talking with others about salvation.

In Ephesus, where Timothy conducted his ministry, the hostility against the Christian faith was severe. So Paul was calling this fledgling pastor to face the enemies of the gospel with courage. And he wrote from a vantage point that demanded attention—Paul himself was suffering in prison for the sake of the gospel. He had discovered that imprisonment was a real part of being a Christ-follower. Christians may not shudder and carefully shy away from conflict with cruel and heartless enemies who want to chew them up and spit them out.

What an encouragement it is to contemplate the nature of the spirit we have been given in place of the natural timidity that takes over whenever Christ's enemies threaten us. The word *spirit* in this instance is written with a lower case *s*, but let there be no mistake that this *s* is here because of God's big *S*. The Holy Spirit, poured out on the church at Pentecost and spread to every living believer, is the one who gives the power, the love, and the self-discipline of which the apostle speaks.

The life of faith is big time. Neither the force of big government, nor that of big business, big friends, or big neighbors can withstand the power that resides in those who trust in Christ. When unbelief works its mischief in believers' hearts, as it sometimes does, they recoil from those who threaten them. But when they are alive in the Word and in prayer and in the fellowship of other Christians, the Christ-Spirit takes over and they express their power, display their love, and exercise the self-discipline that endows their lives with unmistakable holiness.

All this becomes real only for those whose faith is on fire. I cannot expect to be fearless with the courage that results from God's power, love, and holiness unless I have fanned God's gift into a flame. Being a true believer involves fireworks. What God has to give his people is not some kind of religious frosting on an otherwise ordinary cake. "Fan into flame the gift of God," Paul says (2 Tim. 1:6).

The reality of courageous empowerment can be ours when we live terribly close to God through study and contemplation of his Word and through prayer. I say "terribly" because living like this has its "terror" side to it. This is God we are speaking of, and those who earnestly seek him and find him are changed in every fiber of their being.

The spirit of power, love, and self-discipline—why do I not experience it more? Because the flame has died down, and the embers are turning black and cold. O God, fan the flame; give me your fire!

O God, forgive my fear. Take away my timidity. Help me to live close to you through prayer and through the study of your marvelous Word. Send your Holy Spirit into my life so that my faltering spirit may be transformed. May the power I desire not be my own natural power but your power within me; may the love I display be your love within me. Make my life holy with your holiness. Ignite me with the fire of your presence. In Christ, Amen.

Meditation 62

The Mind of the Singer

I will not die, but live. . . .

Psalm 118:17

Sometimes it is difficult for those of one generation to learn the songs of a generation that has different music. So I asked Katie to write out the words of "Lord, I lift your name on high; Lord, I love to sing your praises." I keep it in one of my Bibles now, all printed out in Katie's third-grade hand, wandering across the page a little, a reminder that once Katie and I sang this song together after she taught me the words.

Well, sing this song with Jesus. Psalm 118, I mean—you can sing it with him. One of the fascinating elements of the psalms is that when you read them and the directions for the musicians, you are reading what the people of God sang three thousand or more years ago—and also in Jesus' time. Psalms 113 through 118 were festival psalms used to celebrate the Passover and other high feast times, and this means that when Jesus and his disciples met for Passover, the night before Jesus became the Passover Lamb, they likely sang the words of these psalms.

If you have a spare twenty minutes, read these psalms after you have taken time to pray and compose your mind with the remembrance of Jesus and his disciples singing or reciting them together on the night of betrayal, soon after he had washed his disciples' feet. Each of the persons in that upper room had heard the words often, and the melodies that accompanied them were in their hearts. It was a lot like the singing we do by heart, as when some of us sing "O Jesus, Joy of Loving Hearts" or even "Jesus Loves Me." Once we start the first words of these songs, the rest comes from our hearts, where they are forever lodged. We know these songs. They knew their psalms.

Think of what the words must have meant to Jesus that night. Within hours the salvation that these psalms envisioned would be a reality, but before that would happen he would have to pass through a valley so deep that the fires of hell would sear his body and his soul. As he sang these words, he looked into the faces of the men in that room and knew how sin-filled each of them was, and he knew that he was doing it all for them and for the church that would be built upon their teachings inspired by his Holy Spirit.

What were the thoughts in the God-Man's mind as he took the Spirit-inspired words of Hannah on his lips? It's interesting that 1 Samuel 2:8 found its way into Psalm 113: "He raises the poor from the dust and lifts the needy from the ash heap." Ah, yes, "He settles the barren woman in her home. . . ."

And as Jesus sang of the stupidity of false religion from Psalm 115, did his eye look back across the centuries and far ahead to the year 2000, when his people would continue to battle hideous religious falsehood?

And then, when he sang, "The Lord is with me; I will not be afraid. What can man do to me?" from Psalm 118, did his mind express a fervent prayer to his Father: "O, my Father, you know how fear is there—at the very edge of my consciousness always—please keep it away from me."

And then, "I will not die but live, and will proclaim what the LORD has done. The LORD has chastened me severely, but he has not given me over to death." When he sang that, did Jesus look into the faces of those uncom-prehending men who sat at the table with him and think to himself, "Oh, my dear friends, if you only knew what had to happen before the message of the gospel could be established and proclaimed to the world. If you only knew. But you will never know, not even in eternity when you will know so much more; even then you will never know the depths of love in the Father's heart that made salvation possible."

What was in Jesus' mind as he sang those songs is a divine secret. But we can read these words and marvel at the glory of the salvation Christ has brought to our wretched world. What a grace is here! And what a book we have! It's a songbook that the Savior himself used often, even on the night before he shed his blood for us.

Blessed Savior, forgive us for speculating about something so holy and wonderful. But we want to give our wonderment some substance, so we have tried to think for a few moments about what it must have been like for you to sing those psalms. We trust you understand, dear Jesus. Thank you for dying as you did and for rising for our salvation. In your name, Amen.

Devoted People

They devoted themselves to the apostles' teaching. . . .
Acts 2:42

Woe to those who retire and don't have anything to do afterward!
Undevoted people sometimes collapse completely.

Followers of Christ, however, don't have to collapse because they know
something about devotion. Over the years they become familiar with the
word *devotion,* and when they finally have a little bit of leisure, they are
able to discover what this word means on the deepest level.

Of course, it's possible for us to be devoted to all sorts of things during our
life span. The mother of a nursing baby will be devoted to that baby; her
child is the center of her attention and for several years everything else
about her life is secondary. At certain stages of life, many people will be
fully devoted to achieving skills that will equip them for a specific job. And
there are those whose deep love makes them devoted to each other.

Many who read this are well-acquainted with the idea of *devotion* in connection with books and booklets that guide them to passages of Scripture
and provide them with help as they meditate on a passage each day. These
publications often include a brief prayer that encourages readers to go on
and express their own prayers. Some people customarily use these devotional tools when they have meals together or when they begin or end
their day.

Whatever comes to mind when we think of *devotion,* we cannot experience
the full reality of devotion unless we have the Holy Spirit of God. After all
the excitement of the Pentecostal signs of fire and sound and miraculous
speech, a devoted people became a kind of "holy residue" that remained.

What does the Holy Spirit do to people when he enters their lives? He
makes them devoted people. And those who know devotion on the deepest
level are able to manage even when there are life-changing events like

having your last child go off to kindergarten, losing your job, having to curtail your activity because of a physical problem, or having to adjust to a new environment that you are not particularly enthusiastic about.

There are many people who have nothing to be devoted to. They ricochet through life, spending a little energy on one thing and then another. But those who have received the Holy Spirit of Christ have an endlessly fascinating life. They are able to give themselves with an energizing intensity to activities they know God himself is interested in. They feel themselves in touch with eternity itself.

The idea of devotion that we find in Acts 2:42 is a strong and muscular idea that conveys images of total concentration and focus. Notice the objects of this intense focus: the teaching of the apostles, the fellowship, the breaking of bread, and prayer. When people are captured by the Holy Spirit's power, they are lifted out of themselves and turned away from ordinary preoccupations. They become totally taken in by what is really important.

The teaching of the apostles is the revelation given to the church through the apostles concerning the triune God—Father, Son, and Holy Spirit. The fellowship is the experience of closeness with others who have the Holy Spirit, and the holy meal they celebrate together—the Lord's Supper—binds them to Christ and to fellow believers throughout the world with sacramental power.

Along with all this is the experience of prayer. How can you tell if a person is filled with the Holy Spirit? Ask this: "Is he, is she, devoted to prayer?" This means, of course, that the person spends more than just a brief moment in prayer occasionally throughout the day. A person devoted to prayer practices this holy activity for extended periods of time each day and prays continually in various ways throughout the day.

A devoted person is not one who thinks of God occasionally each day. The Holy Spirit creates people who are devoted to living for God every moment of their lives.

O Holy Spirit, as we think about the explosive power of your entrance into the church, surround our lives and enter our hearts so that we may be devoted to what is truly important. May we arrange our lives and our priorities so that our primary devotion to the good things of your church and kingdom may dominate all we do. In Jesus' name, Amen.

Meditation 64

Seeing God

I will see your face. . . .
Psalm 17:15

There seems to be something deep within a human being that gives rise to expectations of seeing the divine being. Those who have been formed by the revelation given to Moses and the prophets and the apostles know that the day will come when they will behold God, who has revealed himself in Christ.

Psalm 17 concludes with an expression of confidence that the writer will see the face of God and be satisfied. This confidence swept over him in spite of terrifying and miserable circumstances in his life. On the other hand, his confidence may have reached such an intensity not so much *in spite of* all that was going wrong in his life but *because of* it. When our lives are most calamitous, we are often lifted up by marvelous expectations tied to God's promises and sustained by the Bible's message.

When we read the psalms, we often assume that the circumstances of the authors were not entirely different from ours. But they were very different. This psalm was written by a warrior who knew he was in mortal danger. He describes his enemies this way: "They have tracked me down, they now surround me, with eyes alert, to throw me to the ground. They are like a lion hungry for prey, like a great lion crouching in cover" (Ps. 17:11-12).

We associate this psalm with David, whose enemies were legion throughout his life, and even included his own son Absalom at one time. He compares them to a lion lying in wait, and he knew about lions. There are no lions in the wild in Israel today, but they were fairly common when David cared for his sheep. To be sure, he eventually became the king of all Israel, but he was always a realist who knew that he was surrounded by enemies who wanted to kill him.

We have no idea really what it was like to live as he did, like a hunted guerrilla commander with no safety net to catch him when he fell. So it was with all who lived in those days. There was no Medicare then, or Social Security, or disability insurance. People lived from day to day; sometimes they prospered, often they did not. Life was cruel, and enemies often attacked mercilessly and without warning.

But someday I am going to see God—that hope burned in the heart of this hunted man. We can be encouraged by his confidence, but we can also go beyond him. We can have even more confidence. That's because the psalm writer's faith has been transcended by the faith that believers in Christ can have. David lived on the other side of Jesus; we have the vantage point of living after the coming of Jesus and the outpouring of his Holy Spirit.

Now that Jesus has come and has paid the price of sin and secured the victory over death and hell, we may know that we shall surely see him, and we will be satisfied. Yes, Lord, this is true. But even more than this is true. We will also become like him.

Look again at the ending of Psalm 17 and then read this from 1 John 3:2: "We know that when [Jesus Christ] appears, we shall be like him, for we shall see him as he is." The hope that the psalm writer expressed—that he would see God in righteousness and would be satisfied with seeing God's face in the morning—this hope becomes rich and full now that Christ has come and has promised that he will transform us through the power of his Spirit so that one day, in the new heaven and earth, we will be perfect, like him.

Often we are overwhelmed by sickness and suffering. Often we are terrified as we look ahead to the looming threat of pain and misery. We cringe. There is no escape. We advance fearfully. And then those who know Christ remember. There is something beyond the menacing threat—something on the other side of the fearful divide. And that something is God himself. We have been created in his image, and we are going to meet him. Even Old Testament saints sensed that. Now we may have this certainty in a way they could not have it. We are going to see Jesus and, praise God, we will be renewed so that we are like him.

O God, we reach out to you from our place of suffering and sorrow. Often our misery can be so great, our fear so overwhelming and crushing. Thank you for the reminder that we have a brilliant future. We are looking forward to the day when we will see you, O living Christ. Help us live today courageously and with purity as we get ready for that great joy. In your name, Amen.

Parents of Prodigals

His father saw him and was filled with compassion. . . .
Luke 15:20

This is a story for those of us with children who are far from home, not simply in terms of miles, but in terms of a distance between the faith and the values in the parental home and the lack of those things in the life they are living.

When younger parents get together, they often ask, "How's your family—how's Joshua and Ashley?" Parents often ask that of each other when their children are less than ten years old, but when they get into the teens and later, parents are more careful. They become sensitive to the idea that their friends may prefer not to talk about their children. The subject may be too painful. Their children may have become prodigals.

Let's not forget that there's nothing new about this problem of wayward children. When Jesus put the exquisitely heartrending details in the story of the prodigal, it seems as if he had been in some of our homes. Once children start along the wrong path, there's no telling what audacity they will express as they walk away from parental love and control.

"Give me my inheritance *now!*" they may say.

Can you imagine this? Some of us fathers might be tempted to say: "I'll give you your inheritance all right—a good swift kick on your backside. Who do you think you are, anyway?"

So it is. Prodigal children can be so thoughtless, so unappreciative, so cruel. In Jesus' day a son who demanded his inheritance was telling his father that he wished he were dead—a blow of disrespect to the highest degree. That demand may not mean quite the same thing today, but it still shows parents that in their child's eyes they are only good for money or for a roof over their head. It hurts so much to be treated so cruelly by a child you've cared for, prayed for, and had high hopes for. When the rending finally occurs and your child walks away, never to return, it's as if your heart is ripped in two.

But—and this is the mystery—parents and their prodigal children never really disconnect. Never.

One father said to me, "When I hear from him occasionally, I can sort of live with it, and I figure that he will have to go his way, and I will go mine. But when I don't hear from him for weeks and weeks and there is no way I can get in touch with him and I know he's living bad, I realize how connected we are."

God realizes too how connected we are. Jesus realizes it. And he sees those of us whose hearts never seem to heal because a child is far from home.

We may remember also that there is much reason for hope for children who stray far from home—"Train a child in the way he should go, and when he is old he will not turn from it," says the old proverb (Prov. 22:6). Let it be, dear Lord, let it be. But how old does the child have to be before he lives the way he was taught? Yes, there is hope. But that's not really the point of the parable.

The point is that we are prodigal sons and daughters and that our Father in heaven is longing for our return. And God's compassion is infinitely greater than the compassion earthly parents feel for their children who have strayed. We know how we feel when we see our children stumble and rebel. God is watching me this way, every moment, and he knows every time I stray from him.

But none of our disrespect and disobedience changes God's compassion. Those who believe in the Jesus who told this story know that the Father God loves them and will love them forever. Each day, as we turn to him with our prayers of confession and repentance, our Father embraces us anew and welcomes us into his household.

And our love for our prodigals is just a spark from the flame of our Father's love for us.

Father God, have mercy on us, your prodigal children. We confess that we often assume we are living close to you when in fact we are far away. Comfort our broken hearts as we deal with the prodigals we love. And may we remember always that we are prodigals too. Thank you, loving Father, for receiving us in Christ, in whose name we pray, Amen.

Becoming Like God

You may participate in the divine nature. . . .
2 Peter 1:4

Of all the problems we Christian believers have, the greatest is likely that we think of our faith with a perspective far too small. Believing in the Lord Jesus Christ in fact opens our lives to realities that are so magnificent and glorious that we should feel ourselves elevated to glory every moment.

Oftentimes, when life becomes overwhelmingly tragic, we feel we can only weep in our misery. But there should be something within us that lifts us to discover that God has given us so much in the Lord Jesus that our misery cannot extinguish our ever-present rejoicing.

The opening words of 2 Peter tell us what happens when we are joined to God by faith in Christ. We learn in that passage of Scripture that God has made perfect provision "for life and godliness." This provision is not yet another offer of something that promises to lift us out of the limitations of our poor lives—like an offer we might find in our junk mail or on the Internet. It is God's "divine power" that is available to us. When we read a phrase like this, we should realize that we are learning about the greatest power there is.

There's no way we can exhaust that power. In 2 Peter we learn that this power comes to us through the person "who has called us by his own glory and goodness." It's not hard to figure out who that is. Through this entirely satisfactory Savior we can participate in the divine nature and escape the corruption that clings to us like seaweed.

One of the main sources of our misery is the sense we have that when we are sick or depressed or weak, we shouldn't be. We are part of a race created by the Father, Son, and Holy Spirit to be like God, and when God finished with us, he declared us very good. Somewhere within each of us is the sense that we should be perfect. That we are not is a deep source of our anguish.

But believers may be glad to discover that what they have lost has now become their destiny. They are moving toward it, and someday they will be perfect again. Each element of creation has its beauty, but we have more than beauty—we have glory. We are created in God's image to be in a way like God, like Christ the perfect image of God (Rom. 8:29; Heb. 1:3), and now our faith assures us that we already participate in the divine nature.

In his second letter the apostle Peter seems to be saying that today I should be more Christlike than I was yesterday. To be sure, I know that one of these days I am going to die, and then I expect there will be some dramatic changes. But when we remember that Jesus Christ died and rose again in order to give us the Holy Spirit of the living God within us even now, we must expect that already our natures should be undergoing the change to becoming like Christ.

Ideas like these have played a much larger role in the Eastern church than in the Western church, and those who have been captivated by the notion that we become more and more like God while we are in this world have often walked the ascetic road. They have turned away from this world to a degree that they have become strange. They have been willing to be called "God's fools," and the name has fit them.

Must not I be something of an ascetic too, if I participate in the divine nature? How can we escape an affirmative answer to this question? Peter talks about the corruption that comes from evil desires. Surely evil desires are stimulated mightily in this land. The very act of turning on television can confront us with ideas and scenes that are degrading. The evil one has mastered his craft well in this age; he has tools to snare me even while I watch the weather report.

An ascetic? What a queer notion. Who would take it seriously? What could it possibly mean for a savvy, worldly covenant child in this fantastic age? Well, if anything stands between me and realizing the wonder of becoming like God in my life, I may not rest until I find out what that barrier is and seek God's help in getting rid of it.

Thank you, triune God, for giving us everything we need so that we can participate in your divine nature. You have sent your most precious Son into this world to show us what it means to live a Spirit-filled life. On Pentecost you poured out your Spirit like Niagara Falls. Lead me today to the discovery of the fullness of your gifts in me, and help me to cast away whatever keeps me from living for you fully. Through Christ, Amen.

Meditation 67

Gathering Wood

A man was found gathering wood on the Sabbath day.

Numbers 15:32

Among the most jarring events recorded in the Bible, the fate of the hapless Sabbath woodgatherer is high on the list. If punishment should fit the crime, there seems to be something seriously amiss here. Gathering wood is hardly a capital offense. In this case a man was executed for doing that, and our shock is compounded by the announcement that the Lord himself passed the sentence.

When it comes to the Sabbath, we much prefer a report of the Lord's reaction to Sabbath questions found in Mark 2, where Jesus replies to another query about how the Sabbath should be observed. Mark tells us that Jesus' disciples were guilty of conduct as perverse as that of the woodgatherer in Numbers 15. One Sabbath the disciples picked heads of grain and popped them into their mouths as they walked with Jesus through grainfields. The religious leaders, who saw them do this and who had surely discussed the woodgatherer a time or two, figured they had caught the disciples red-handed. But Jesus, who we believe to be the same God as the one who passed sentence on the man in Numbers, rejected the accusations and announced a principle that stands to this day: "The Sabbath was made for man, not man for the Sabbath. So the Son of Man is Lord even of the Sabbath" (Mark 2:27-28).

There's a mystery here that cannot be denied, and no amount of talk can cover it up. There's an appalling side to the Lord's insistence that the woodgathering Sabbath desecrator be stoned to death—and swiftly. The punishment seems crude and barbaric to us because there are several realities operating here that have gone off our radar screen.

For one thing, we don't realize that God is creating a new people here out of a slave nation that needed to be taught, often in a most dramatic manner, that when God told them something, he meant it. And God had prohibited any work on the Sabbath. Another thing we don't have sensitivity for anymore is the marvel of the covenant of grace that God put in place, promising that he would be the people's saving God. And the Sabbath was the sign of that covenant. Woodgathering on the Sabbath at that time was a rejection of God's covenant mercy. The death sentence served to announce that those who stepped outside the circle of divine mercy stepped into a realm in which they met God's wrath.

Such considerations help us to understand such events to some degree. The fact remains, though, that the same God who exonerated the disciples killed a man several centuries before for not keeping the Sabbath. How should we respond to this?

First of all, these events, taken together, affirm the extraordinary significance of the Sabbath principle. With the coming of Jesus, the Sabbath prohibitions fall away, and the Sabbath as a splendid gift to humankind emerges in full brilliance. The Sabbath is the gift of communion with God. It is there for us on the festive day of rest when we gather with God and his people; it is there for us always because the way between humanity and God has been cleared and rendered smooth by the Lord of the Sabbath, Jesus Christ. Gather wood if it pleases you; shine your shoes if you must; even iron your shirt if necessary—and, yes, strip an ear of corn and let the juice of the enzyme-rich kernels satisfy your hunger.

But as you use the Sabbath, remember that it is a fearsome blessing, as the sad fate of the woodgatherer still attests. While it may be true that we need no longer treat the Sabbath with abject fear that God's wrath might suddenly destroy us for some desecration, it remains true that Sabbath observance is a matter of life and death.

Those who ignore worship as if their life and pleasure depend only on their own effort will find their lives plagued by strange maladies. We neglect the Lord's Sabbath to our detriment. It remains the blessed covenant sign, and those who learn the sweet discipline of honoring the Sabbath from the depths of their Spirit-filled heart are blessed immeasurably.

Covenant-keeping God, teach us what it means to enjoy the special day you have given us. Free us from the compulsion to work and play every day as if our lives depended on our efforts. We confess our own "woodgathering," showing a lack of respect for your covenant love for us, and we ask your forgiveness. Make our Sabbaths beautiful and holy and please put some Sabbath into every day for us. For Jesus' sake, Amen.

The Worry Hour

Do not be anxious about anything.

Philippians 4:6

"If you have trouble sleeping and it's worry that's making you sleepless, stop worrying in the middle of the night. Here's how. Do your worrying during the day. Set aside one hour each day exclusively for worrying. Take care of your worrying then, and when it comes up at 2:00 a.m., set it aside until your worry hour."

I laughed when I heard a broadcaster make this suggestion. It's an intriguing idea, but it won't work. Worry cannot be neatly packaged and assigned to sixty minutes after lunch, or whenever. And if you have a bad case of worries, it tends to spill over and contaminate every hour. Sorry, Mr. Broadcaster, but I'm not even going to try your suggestion.

Worry is among our most distressing problems, and all of us are bothered by it at one time or another. When the time we are bothered is the middle of the night, worry can drive us to distraction. It can plunge us into the depths of depression. If there's a way to overcome it, we'd sure like to find out.

It is impressive how much of the Bible deals with worry and with the fact that we shouldn't worry. In the Sermon on the Mount Jesus spends a fair bit of time dealing with the issue (Matt. 6:25-34). He says to his followers, in effect, "There's no reason for you to worry. It won't help anything. It's futile. And, besides, it's superfluous: your heavenly Father knows your needs, and he will take care of you—you can be sure of that."

Building on these ideas found in Matthew 6:25-34, the apostle Paul tells us to worry about nothing whatsoever. But that might strike us as strange, especially since Paul himself has been known to be a bit upset and worried a time or two. (Look at 1 Thessalonians 3:1, 5, which shows that the apostle seems to be extremely agitated.) What really does Paul have in mind here? The word he uses means in some cases "to have concern for," as in

1 Corinthians 7:32, where he says he wants people to be "concerned about the Lord's affairs. . . ." In Philippians 4:6, however, Paul is using the word the way Jesus did in the Sermon on the Mount. Paul is talking about the paralyzing, crippling, overpowering, exasperating, terrifying worry that makes us basket cases during the day and humorless insomniacs at night.

This is serious—worry is very serious indeed; it can raise your blood pressure and your cholesterol and tear your immune system to pieces. Setting aside one hour each day for this ghastly activity is impossible, and if it were, who would deliberately arrange for such a dismal sixty minutes?

But there is a remedy. Believers in Christ, who are filled with the Spirit of Christ, can indeed have a special hour they use to combat worry. Actually for them it's an anti-worry hour. It is that special time they set aside for prayer. Prayer is the opposite of worry.

"Do not be anxious about anything, but in everything, by prayer and petition, with thanksgiving, present your requests to God." That's it. The words are simple and easy to understand. But it takes great faith to put them into practice. There is an absoluteness here—don't be anxious about *anything*. Don't worry. Don't worry. Instead pray. Pray.

And we must offer our prayers with thanksgiving. How can you set worry aside and surrender yourself and your fate to God entirely? Only when you look back at God's track record. Look what he has done for you. "He who did not spare his own Son, but gave him up for us all—how will he not also, along with him, graciously give us all things?" (Rom. 8:32).

And God's track record is the only one that extends into the future. We have the record of what he did, and we have his promises of what he will do—and God's promises are as good as done.

It's not easy to surrender everything to God with thanksgiving. Is that really true? It is easy in faith. In faith we can do this. We need to flex our faith, use it, put it on the NordicTrac. Believe that God will take care of us. Believe it. And don't worry about anything.

Father in heaven, make this freedom from worry real for us. We really do consider ourselves Christians—we believe in you. Why do we worry so much? We know the answer: it's because of our weak faith. Strengthen our faith. Help us to cast all our burdens on you with the certainty that just as you have taken care of us in the past, you'll continue to do so. In Christ, Amen.

No Place to Lean

Lean not on your own understanding. . . .
Proverbs 3:5

The incredible advance of knowledge we now experience implies that we all are becoming more and more intelligent and wise. The very way people talk about smartness and ability these days is quite different from what it was fifty years ago. Most of our knowledge then was contained in books, and the wisest and the best knew the philosophers and great literature. They also knew something about Christianity, even about the great classics—the Fathers, the writings of Aquinas and Calvin, and the Bible itself.

Today knowledge is viewed in terms of information that helps us accomplish things; it rearranges our world and provides us with powerful tools we can use to "get the job done." It's all there on our hard drives, our CD-ROMs, and the Internet. We rely on the enormous availability of knowledge in medicine, business, and agriculture to help us make it through. Philosophy and religion, on the other hand—what use are they? And the great religious classics—what difference do they really make?

Those of us who still want to live by the sacred Scriptures feel that something deadly is gradually moving in on us, an institutionalized disdain of anything that claims the Bible as its unshakable authority. It's almost embarrassing to notice, when perusing the book of Proverbs, that human understanding will always let you down. In Proverbs 3 we find a sentence that many preachers have used in the past when they were asked to address a graduating class. "Hey, all you smart dudes," the preacher might say, "don't forget that when push comes to shove, trusting in God with all your heart is more important than everything you learned in this school. Even if you're the valedictorian that doesn't make any difference: 'Trust in the Lord with all your heart and lean not on your own understanding; in all your ways acknowledge him, and he will make your paths straight'" (Prov. 3:5-6). Would I dare use that Scripture today?

We are rapidly moving into the same situation Russia used to be in (and may be returning to once again): when Lenin's wife was the head of the Russian educational system, she figured that it would only be a matter of time before everyone would understand that trusting in the Lord is nonsense. And she worked hard to make that happen. Today we run our businesses, milk the cows in our milk factories, and figure out how our pancreases are doing primarily in terms of the knowledge we now have. We're so smart that we're dumb.

The humbling reality is that everyone who wants to do the will of God must trust in God rather than lean on his or her own understanding. This means that the God who revealed himself in the Bible must be the center of our lives. It means that we must not spend so much time at our computers and other interests that we have no time to pray to God and to read and reflect on his Word.

It's possible for some who cannot shake off the influence of Christian tradition to continue to express such pious acts without fully trusting in God. The weight and prestige of the current explosion of knowledge is so overwhelming that we are always tempted to pray and study the Word as a religious exercise without making these the most determinative things we do.

The statement we are looking at in Proverbs 3 is about where we let our weight fall, what we depend on for our day-by-day decisions. For those of us who have developed some expertise in a certain field, it doesn't take much to convince us that we are invincible in that field. Leaning on one's own understanding is the most natural thing in the world. Why would we not do it?

Those of us who are older know that the places in our lives where we have leaned with all our weight on our own understanding are the places we have failed. "In retrospect," we say, "that was not a good decision." Or we say, with a wry smile, "Hindsight is 20/20 vision." True enough. But these little comments don't cut through to the heart. We must say, "I was proud; I thought I understood. I leaned on my own understanding. And that is no place to lean. When will I ever learn to acknowledge God and trust him so that he will make my ways straight?"

Yes, it is true, O God, we really find it very hard to trust you fully and to await your direction in our lives. We feel we know so much that most of the elements of our lives no longer require dependence on you. Help us to examine our lives in all honesty so that we will discern just how mistaken we often are. Please make our paths straight. In Jesus' name, Amen.

The Death Escape

"Whoever . . . believes in me will never die."
John 11:26

If you see a sign at a signal light that says, "No turn on red," you take it seriously. If, however, you saw a sign that said, "No go on green," you'd figure something was wrong. You might laugh. Most likely when the light turned green, you'd go anyway. You'd figure the sign was a mistake; it just couldn't be right.

We are apt to react the same way to what Jesus says here. "Never die?" we say. "This can't be right. Yes, it's there in the Bible, but someone must have made a mistake." So we go on and figure on dying, though Jesus said we wouldn't if we believe while we live.

What can we do to make this teaching of Jesus sink in? Here we have the best news we could possibly receive, and something in us refuses to think and act in the light of this exciting statement.

What Jesus is saying here is very simple. He is standing at the tomb of one of his best friends, Lazarus, whose sister is aggravated with Jesus because he hasn't come sooner. If only he had come sooner, her brother wouldn't be wrapped up in grave clothes in a stinking cave. Jesus knows, but Martha doesn't, that within days he is going to accomplish a magnificent victory over death that will make eternal life absolutely sure for all his people.

Jesus says, "I am the resurrection and the life. He who believes in me will live, even though he dies; and whoever lives and believes in me will never die." Then he asks Martha—and you and me—in effect, "Tell me now, do *you* really believe this?"

The message is simple: if a person believes in Jesus, that person will never die. Jesus makes this clear by saying it two ways: *the person will live even though he or she dies,* and *whoever lives and believes in Jesus will never die*. And we might say, "Sure, sure, I know—but what about all those believers lying in caskets? They're dead as a doornail."

Yes, that's true. Our bodies—they shrivel up and get wrinkled and baggy on the outside. And who knows what's happening on the inside? Arthritis, diabetes, lupus, MS, Mr. Gehrig's disease. And accidents—they can be horrible. And wars—some of us remember wars that brought slaughter to entire towns and killed young men in the prime of life. Yes, we die. We shall all die.

True, our bodies will. But, if you believe in Jesus as your Savior—you, that is—*you* will not. And who are you? You are that person who is in the middle of all these things we have been looking at. But somewhere in the midst of that body that is vulnerable to accident, war, disease, and aging, there's an indestructible person. And that person will live forever before the face of God in glory. That's what Jesus is saying.

Death is the final scarecrow. We see it up ahead, flapping its arms at us and mocking us with its hideous face. But we believe in Christ. He strode into death's maw and faced a horror that we cannot even comprehend because our little minds cannot understand what it means to "taste death for everyone" (Heb. 2:9).

Everyone thinks about death at some time. We cannot avoid doing that. So if we are truly Christians, let's begin by taking Jesus fully seriously as he speaks to us from the tombsite. We do not know much about what is on the other side for us, but if we believe Christ is our Savior, one thing we may know for sure is that we will be the same persons on the other side of the grave as we are on this side.

Oh, poor bodies! Watch them go. It is inevitable. And sometimes when pathetic disease embraces us, we gasp in terror and look wide-eyed at one another and ask, "What is it going to be like?"

Jesus says, "I can't tell you now, but just remember this: you are going to pass right on through to glory. *You* will. The real you, the basic you, the fundamental you, the essential you. *You* will never die."

O Jesus, may your good news to us sink in. Make it penetrate our thick skulls. As we hear this good news today, don't let us figure there must be some mistake. Fill us with inexpressible gladness as we remember that your victory is our victory. O Lord, your words make this day look so much different than it would otherwise. Thank you, Jesus, Amen.

This Blessed Nation

Blessed are the people whose God is the LORD.

Psalm 144:15

Children of the church still like to sing "Onward Christian Soldiers," though some of us who are older cringe because we have become more sensitive to the overpowering military ideas that dominate the song. Do we really need to think of ourselves as "soldiers marching as to war"?

Yes. Although there's much good in a peaceful demeanor among Christian people, to our peril we abandon biblical figures of speech drawn from military operations. Psalm 144 is one example among many that shows that imagery drawn from warfare is an integral part of biblical religion.

From Abraham's day onward, the people of God were surrounded by enemies. And a majority of the psalms derive their vigorous power from the fact that they were composed in the presence of their foes. David, who wrote many of them, was a guerrilla commander and army general. There were times when he was the victim of vicious treachery; at one time one of his own sons became his archenemy.

The enemies of God's people described in Scripture were not merely those who for whatever reason wanted Israel's real estate, but they were those whose religion was opposed to the true religion of Jahweh, the only true God. Israel had not chosen Jahweh willy-nilly; rather, he had chosen them. As his covenant people—those with whom God had a special relationship— they had dreadful enemies; God's enemies became their enemies.

If that was true in the days in which David wrote Psalm 144, it remains true today—or perhaps we should say that it is becoming more and more true again. A superficial examination of the centuries leading up to this one reveals Western civilization largely under the influence of ideas that came from Christianity. Today, those ideas are being jettisoned, and a ruthless pluralism is taking its place. Pluralism—or cultural relativism, which is similar—declares that there is no religion that can claim exclusive truth. All are viewed as equally valuable paths to truth.

When people exchange the principles of Christianity for New Age principles or for those of other religions such as Islam and Buddhism, those people and their nation deteriorate. But God's people are blessed. As Psalm 144 concludes, it describes a near idyllic situation: here we see a nation whose sons are "like well-nurtured plants," whose daughters are "like pillars carved to adorn a palace." It is a nation in which the "barns will be filled with every kind of provision." There will be abundance of livestock. The general condition of the land that follows the true God will be one of unshakable security: "There will be no breaching of walls, no going into captivity, no cry of distress in our streets."

Such wholesome and peaceable circumstances cannot be achieved along a political road. They do not attend the platform of one political party in contrast to another. Such circumstances arise only among those people whose God is the Lord.

And who are they? Can they be identified with one country or another, such as Finland? Or Chad? David, nationalistic as he was, was not talking about a country as such. He was talking about a people, the covenant people of God. These are people who know the true God, who delight in knowing his will, and who want nothing more than to serve him.

Where do we find this nation today? It's not on the map. But it exists wherever the people of God live and work together. The covenant people today exist wherever there are those who faithfully follow Jesus Christ. Such people express their faith within their churches, but you cannot describe them solely in terms of what goes on within their churches. Their faith in Christ their Lord goes far beyond what happens when they are met in worship. It affects everything they do. It makes their marriages, their homes, their families, their schools, their way of life uniquely holy and peace-filled. You find this nation—these people—within many nations. Also in the United States and Canada.

O Lord, we do have enemies yet today. We ask for your protection. Though we live in a hostile environment, may we feel your power lifting us up and caring for us. May we show through our marriages, families, schools, and daily work that you are our God. And, if it be your will, surround us with the bounties of your favor—not because we deserve it but for Jesus' sake, Amen.

Conditions for Fruit-bearing

The desires for other things . . . choke the word. . . .
Mark 4:19

One of the biggest problems I have when I read the Bible is that there is so much in it that I assume applies to other people. When I assume that, a lot of it just slides right past me without shaking me at all. That's certainly the case with the parable of the sower.

It's a really difficult parable to preach on. I've tried to do it, and I have had students try. The students have made the same mistake I have. What a preacher will do with this story is describe the three defective kinds of people upon whom the seed falls. One kind is like the macadam of the highway; one kind is like a rocky path; and one kind is like a briar patch. Then there's also the kind that's like a newly plowed Iowa field in the spring. I always assumed I was like the Iowa field.

When you finish describing these, what do you say to the people you're preaching to? Do you say, "Okay, which kind of person are you?" Go figure. Or do you say, "Make sure you're not like one of the first three kinds of soil?" If you're a Calvinist preacher, how could you say that? After all, doesn't God determine what kind of person you are? Usually I have sort of concluded, "Well, this story tells us how the mission of the Lord works, and it explains why not everyone responds in faith. Amen." It's pretty hard to make a personal application here, other than to be thankful you're like an Iowa field—if you really are, that is.

Why is it so hard to make a personal application of this parable? One day it came to me. This story is not about God's mission; it's about production. It's about being a productive Christian. Peter once wrote about avoiding the danger of becoming "ineffective and unproductive" Christians (2 Pet. 1:8). And when I recognized this, the entire story hit me in the solar plexus.

This story shows me why I am not more productive. Now, the idea of being productive does not refer to how many sermons a preacher makes or how many Sunday school lessons a teacher teaches. It refers to whether or not people experience the kingdom of God because of you. There are people nowadays whom God uses marvelously; there are entire denominations whose theology is full of holes but who are bearing fruit faster than they can keep up with it. The third kind of soil is the one that really stops *me* dead in my tracks once I see that this parable is about productivity; I fit the profile of the thorny-place person. This kind of person hears the word of God—and yet worry, wealth, and desires for things make the word unfruitful by choking it. Worry, wealth, and wants break the holy chain of hearing, accepting, and producing. Here is one of Jesus' ironclad, unbreakable rules for spiritual health. Ignore this and you will be a sterile believer who may sing "And Can It Be" with gusto but who won't bear any fruit.

Hearing the word, accepting it, and bearing fruit can happen only when the seed of the Word of God becomes the dominant power in a person's life. It must be so powerful and overwhelming that it neutralizes worry, wealth, and desires for things. If it isn't that powerful, then worry, wealth, and desires will kill it just as effectively as what happens when Satan comes and takes away the word sown next to the highway.

This teaching does not necessarily apply to someone else; I must allow myself to be shaken by it. Once again, I learn that authentic Christianity is a matter of what is going on in the depths of my heart. Worrying, enjoying wealth, and desiring other things is something that can become so much a part of our lives that we consider it entirely natural.

How can we tell if a person is right deep inside, whether a person has heard the Word of God and accepted it to the point where everything else is thrust into the background? The fruit tells the story. The fruit is the litmus test. Productivity shows what's really going on in the heart of a believer, in the hearts of members of a church . . . of a denomination.

I must try to preach on this once again; maybe I will finally get it right. If I do, it will have to be a confession of my own sin.

O glorious storyteller, you tell frightening tales. Yes, I know, they are designed to reveal the truth to some people and to hide it from others. Forgive me for thinking so long that the farmer story didn't really apply to me. Help me to see how inclined I am to be involved in worry and riches and wanting things. O Lord, change me. In your name, Amen.

Meditation 73

The Great Bypass

There were shepherds living out in the fields. . . .
Luke 2:8

The huge billboard along the expressway jars me with its announcement "THERE'S A BYPASS AHEAD." That's about all it says besides identifying the large hospital that sponsors this sign. I assume that when I need bypass surgery, the doctors will be ready. And I may need a bypass someday, just as many people do. Bypasses are necessary when something blocks off the blood that the heart and body need to stay functioning; when that happens, a surgeon reroutes the blood flow around the blocked area, through a vein taken from the patient's leg or through some other kind of tube.

What is so humbling for people who have long been a part of the church is that God often uses bypasses to get his mission accomplished. You'd think that the church would always be the conduit through which divine grace would flow to those who need it, but there are times when religious people get in the way of the very processes they are supposed to be promoting. I guess we shouldn't be surprised, though, because at the very beginning of this era, God used an astonishing bypass to carry his mission forward.

That's really what happened when Jesus was born and God ignored the entire religious establishment and put on a heavenly display of glory for shepherds. If we were not so all-fired used to the story of Christ's coming, we would realize how remarkable it was that shepherds heard the message first. But it's not just because we are so accustomed to the story of Christ's coming that we fail to notice how unusual it was that shepherds played a leading role at the time of his birth. The image we carry around in our minds of shepherds is so idealized, even romanticized, that it doesn't help us realize what Luke describes in his account of Christ's birth. We think of shepherds in terms of Psalm 23 and the "good shepherd" idea. The reality is that when Jesus was born the very idea of a "good shepherd" was an oxymoron. People figured you could no more have a good shepherd than you could have a good case of the flu.

Shepherds were a despised class—for at least two reasons. First of all, they were always in a state of ceremonial uncleanness. They just couldn't do what had to be done to be fully acceptable religiously. Second, and possibly because of the first reason, they had a reputation for stealing stuff. People figured that since they were ceremonially unclean, you couldn't trust them, and some shepherds concluded that, since most of the people considered them scoundrels, they might as well act that way. This is what *The Geneva Study Bible* tells us about shepherds.

Now, with this background in mind as you think of what happened when Jesus was born, isn't it mind-boggling that God chose these despicable scoundrels to receive the news of the Savior's birth? God bypassed all the religious establishment—the scribes, the Pharisees, the teachers of the law, and the high priest—and tore the dark of that night apart with heaven's brilliance to tell the message of Jesus' birth to shepherds. And those shepherds did what needed to be done. They didn't have any books to consult. They didn't have to check with any higher-ups. They just said, "Hey, let's get over Bethlehem and check this out—right now!" Boom, they were on their way, and they were the very first of millions and millions of people after them to worship the Christchild.

I don't expect that these men were among the most verbal in the world. Despised, suspected of stealing, often spending days on end away from ordinary society, they didn't talk much. But God transformed them into the first communicators of the gospel. They told people what they had seen and heard. And they returned to their fields, glorifying and praising God.

Humble shepherds humble us. So many of us have our assigned places in the church. We have a job to do, and we want to do it well. But often we get in the way of grace. And then God comes and creates a bypass. He is still doing that, and when it happens seasoned old Christians whose reputations are the gold standard just have to step aside and marvel at God's gracious way of getting his job done.

Almighty God, give us self-knowledge that will enable us to get out of the way if we are blocking your grace. So often we think we are furthering your kingdom when really we are building our own. Lord, you can use anyone to get your job done, even despised shepherds. May we realize this and praise you when you construct a bypass. In Christ, Amen.

The Prayer Teacher

"Lord, teach us to pray. . . ."
Luke 11:1

Prayer is so common among both believers in the true God and believers in false gods that we are not startled by Luke's record of Jesus' teaching his disciples to pray. But we should be startled. More than that: just meditating on this prayer-teaching episode can put us in touch with about everything there is to know about the Christian faith.

The disciples' request is not surprising; they wanted to have a trademark prayer just as John's disciples had—a prayer that would identify them as those who followed Christ, not some other rabbi. But Jesus' answer should startle us. He said he would teach them to pray. And Jesus was and is God. In Jesus' positive response to the disciples' request, God was responding to them.

Because Jesus is God, he could have responded differently. He could have told the disciples they were not allowed to pray because of their sin. Or he could have told them gently that they need not spend time (waste time?) praying because, in all honesty, God had everything already planned and that he would do what he would do no matter what. But Jesus didn't talk that way. He taught his disciples the perfect prayer we have come to call the Lord's Prayer.

When we read the Lord's Prayer, we discover that in it God does not abdicate his own right and power to run the universe; notice that the prayer even describes temptations as events that occur within the circle of God's will. Jesus' instruction in the fine art of praying is an announcement that God has chosen to allow us to participate in his running of the universe.

It's hard to know what kind of prayer the disciples were expecting to learn, but more than likely they didn't have in mind what Jesus gave them. "Pray," Jesus said, "that your Father's kingdom may come and that his will may be done on earth as it is in heaven." Now, there's no question that this is going to happen anyway. Everything in the Bible indicates that God's will is supreme and cannot be opposed or turned aside. True enough. Yet God is pleased to exercise his will in response to his peoples' prayers.

With this prayer Jesus announces that the sovereign God who rules all has elevated us to an exalted position within the universe. He will do as he wills to do. But the God who will do as he wills to do also delights in incorporating his children into the accomplishment of his will.

To be sure, he encourages us to pray for the necessities of our lives when he tells us to pray for "bread," which represents every material thing we need for our physical well-being. But this prayer goes far beyond that. Jesus invites us to pray for exalted realities.

The coming of God's kingdom—we are invited to be much in prayer for that. And worldwide obedience to his will—we are invited to pray for that. When the kingdom comes in all its final glory, we will be able to rejoice— not only because of the wonder of it but also because it will come in answer to our prayers. Whenever we observe anyone earnestly seeking to do the will of God, we may rejoice because that is an answer to our prayers.

And with the prayer Jesus taught, he swung the focus of our lives around toward righteousness and goodness. We are to pray for moral rectitude more than for bread. This prayer portrays us as warriors on a moral battle-field, and the battles are waged within our hearts.

Everybody prays, we're told—even atheists. But the prayers of the followers of Christ are unique—let's call them *Christprayers*. To pray to God in Christ's name and to pray in a way that replicates the pattern of his holy teaching lifts us high above all that customarily goes by the name of prayer. Redeemed people, whose minds have been transformed by Christ's Spirit, become God's companions. Their goals are God's goals. Their will is God's will. Their Christ-taught and Spirit-directed prayers are the calls God delights to respond to as he does his will and establishes his kingdom.

Thank you, holy Teacher, for not turning your disciples away when they asked for help in prayer. We are awed as we contemplate your desire that we pray and that you even give us a template we can use as we seek to pray acceptably. Conform our will to yours, O Christ, and give us great joy as we observe your answer to our prayers to the glory of our Father. In your name, Amen.

Watching Fathers

"While he was still a long way off, his father saw him. . . ."
Luke 15:20

I heard a pastor tell other pastors that if he ever had a child who was an unbeliever, he would leave the ministry. He felt that this was the meaning of Titus 1:6, which says that the only men who can be elders are those whose children believe. I know the passage. But I also know Jesus' story. I asked that pastor, "If the father of the prodigal son were an elder, should he resign from his office?"

"Yes," he said.

That pastor's view presents a distressing problem. If his rule were suddenly put into place, probably half of the church's elders and ministers over forty years of age would have to resign. If we remember that this parable reveals Jesus' mind to us—God's mind actually—we should look at it to see how God looks at such problems. When we do that, we discover that the father in the story is an "expectant" father. Yes, there are expectant fathers, just as there are expectant mothers.

Of this we can be certain: the most obnoxious behavior of a child cannot destroy a father's loving heart. In the story Jesus told, the father's younger son had treated him shamefully and disrespectfully. The man's son had disgraced him. Others had been watching, and among them was the man's elder son. That son knew that his kid brother had actually robbed their father, taking what did not belong to him while his father was alive.

Notice too that the father did not give up on his younger son. As devastating as it was for him as a father, he seemed to recognize that it was a passing phase in his son's life. So he left the door of the house open. As he went about his ordinary business, it was as if he would frequently take a glance toward the doorway to see if his son had come back. And there were times when he would watch along the road his son had taken when he left.

Often when this story is discussed in church, the point is made that what we have here is a picture of our Father God—and that doubtlessly is true. But what flows from Jesus' mind here is also a description of an ordinary father. When Jesus thinks about fathers, this is one of the duties he assigns them: never giving up on their wandering children and always watching, ready to welcome them when they return.

Almost everyone who knows anything about the Bible knows the details that Jesus puts into his description of the scoundrel son's return. The son delivers the pathetic speech he had rehearsed, acknowledging his sin and begging for a place on the payroll, if not at his father's table. And so on. It's all there for any of us to read. It's beautiful. The main thing is that the father simply receives his son—after all that he had done—just as if none of it had happened. Then they have a great celebration.

All the little details Jesus puts into this story support the idea that when wandering sons return to their fathers, they will find an openhearted welcome. Now, this all gets rather complicated in terms of the actual situations some of us may be thinking about in our own lives. Is it true that fathers should be able to take all the wrong that has happened and act as if it never happened? Hey, just a minute—is it really that way?

Well, Jesus says it is. Surely we should conclude from all this that we must be a lot more forgiving than we are . . . a lot more. And if we have trouble thinking about this in terms of our own lives, isn't it surpassingly encouraging to be able to think about it in terms of us and our relationship to our Father in heaven? Yes, Jesus is talking about earthly fathers here, but it is true that above and beyond them is the heavenly Father and that we are prodigal children.

When dead and lost prodigals are changed by God's Holy Spirit and they head for home, the Father God is there watching them come. And he has been watching and waiting for them all the time. When we fathers—and mothers—look into Jesus' mind and heart, we learn how we should act, and we—prodigals all—are encouraged to return to our heavenly Father, who is waiting for our return.

Storytelling Savior, thank you for telling us this touching story. Now come into our hearts with your Holy Spirit so that we may be the kind of parents we should be. Help us to be wise and loving with our children. And help us to remember that we are children too, children who often stray and must return to you, our God. Thank you for receiving us when we come back home. In Jesus' name, Amen.

Meditation 76

The Whereabouts of Faith

"Where is your faith?"
Luke 8:25

From Jesus' point of view, the faith we think we have isn't worth much unless it is activated by calamity. Most of us figure we have faith in God; we say the Apostles' Creed with some enthusiasm and have passed the faith test required for becoming members of the church we attend. That's a good start. But the litmus test of my faith's value is where it is when I lose control of my life and tomorrow threatens to be more terrifying than today.

The two biblical episodes that display Jesus' total control of a wild sea have this element in common: the Bible's intent seems to point more toward the revelation of how deficient the disciples' faith was than toward the display of Christ's power.

The sea-calming miracle of Luke 8 occurred during a fairly routine squall on the Sea of Galilee; the other one occurred after Jesus walked on water to the aid of his struggling disciples—in that instance, Peter had walked on water to meet Jesus and had sunk beneath the waves when the fury of the tempest got the best of him. Jesus did not sympathize with Peter and assure him that he understood his terror. Instead he rebuked him: "You of little faith . . . why did you doubt?" (Matt. 14:31).

When we examine the storm-stilling episodes in the New Testament, the impression we get is that Jesus has little patience with disciples whose faith vanishes whenever there's real trouble. So long as events are fairly ordinary, most believers do not have much trouble giving the illusion of trusting in Christ. But storms can cause that trust to vanish and other elements of our lives to take over.

We might expect Jesus to be more understanding. Those of us who have experienced an ocean storm wonder why people want to go on cruises for enjoyment. One fierce December night at sea, I stumbled out of my bunk and staggered down a careening passageway to find the source of a mighty crash I'd heard; I found the sea blowing through the "watertight" door on the vessel's side, and when I reached the deck, the towering waves and wind, just one notch below hurricane force, made me cringe in fear. How ironic it would have been to go down in the Atlantic there, not more than a hundred miles out of New York—but it could have happened.

If I had met him then, Jesus would not have said, "I can understand why you're scared." He would have shouted above the storm, "Where is your faith?"

Faith isn't worth much if it's only good for a cruise. The stormy Galilee is a symbol of the catastrophes that can sweep in upon us and change everything in an instant. Calamity can come in a phone call, a consultation with a physician, a letter. Intimations of calamity can come in a strange pain that develops deep within your rib cage, across the top of your belly or in your groin—a spot, a lump—these can put faith into a tailspin.

Once I heard a young Korean seminarian talk about his own despair as he wrestled with rheumatoid arthritis. "My knees became as big as soccer balls," he said, and the doctors could not diagnose his disease. He prayed; his friends prayed. After three months in a wheelchair, he was given a medicine that brought relief. He concluded, "Whether we will experience suffering is not the question. The question is, 'Where is our faith when suffering comes?'"

The whereabouts of faith is the important issue.

Jesus had given his disciples enough evidence that he was totally in control. They had seen his miracles. They had even heard him forgive sins. They should have known. They should have believed.

We now live this side of his resurrection and his ascension. Jesus has done more than walk on water; he has walked through hell to a victory that includes the rescue of everyone who believes in him. When calamity comes, I must trust him. Trust him. That's the litmus test. The question is not whether I have faith in Christ but whether I trust in him even when the time of testing comes. And with his help I certainly can.

All-powerful Savior, you have given us faith, but often we fail to live as faith-filled people. Be with us as we are overwhelmed by towering waves and terrifying tempests. It's easy to talk; it's harder to trust you in every situation. As we journey toward our ultimate dread, prepare us even now so that then and until then, our faith will remain firm. In your name and by your Spirit, Amen.

Meditation 77

The Hubble and Genesis

In the beginning God created. . . .
Genesis 1:1

Now that the Hubble Space Telescope is out there, 370 miles from the earth, we have to read Genesis differently. If Genesis is about the same subject the Hubble is about, we just have to lay flat-out in worship more than ever.

There are some who say that the Hubble and Genesis shouldn't be discussed on the same page. Genesis, they say, is a religious/faith description of creation written by people whose knowledge of the cosmos was virtually nil. The Hubble Space Telescope, in contrast, provides us with actual pictures of what really happened when the universe came into existence.

Genesis is about what the Hubble is about—it's a declaration that announces that God has made every galaxy and that every cosmic event is under his control. Some Christians believe that God made everything in six twenty-four-hour days. That's what the Bible says, though the twenty-four-hour span is not stated as such. I too believe the Bible—now more than ever. And I believe that what the Hubble is finding is forcing me not so much to readjust my view of Genesis but to readjust my faith in God.

Sharon Begley wrote an article about the Hubble that contained stunning photographs of colliding galaxies, of six-trillion-mile-high fingers of hydrogen gas and dust, of black holes, and of a supernova. She tells us that these are images of events that happened billions of years ago and that it is entirely incorrect to think, as the seventeenth-century Irish archbishop James Ussher declared, that creation occurred in 4004 B.C. Creation actually occurred 13 billion to 14 billion years ago, writes Sharon.

I can understand why those who view the Hubble photos start talking about 13 billion and more years; I can understand that when stars move away from us, they turn more red, and that we can use some of them to make a calculation about when the universe began. But such calculations depend on lots of presuppositions. They would be wrong, for example, if, when God created the stars, he also created their light connection with earth at the same time. Scientists will laugh when they read this. But that's all right. I have vast ignorance when it comes to origins, but they do too.

For those of us who believe that Genesis and the Hubble are connected, it should be very clear that the simple words that open the Bible are about events far more astounding than I ever thought back in seventh grade. There is something here that we cannot expect a Sunday school teacher to get across. When we say God is the Creator, we are declaring a fact so transcendently wonder-filled that we really don't know what we are talking about.

The Hubble is showing us a view of the greatness of God that lays us prostrate before his divinity. "The heavens declare the glory of God" (Ps. 19:1). But for those who believe Genesis 1, the full wonder is that there is so much more to the Bible. The Bible not only announces that the God of Abraham, Isaac, and Jacob is the creator God and that all other gods are idols, but it also reveals that the fullness of God's glory is not expressed in the cosmos he has made. The fullness of God's glory is expressed in his character.

God is worthy of our praise not only because he has made this breathtaking cosmos but also because he is holy. He is an ethical being who is love. The Creator God is the holy, loving God. And even this is not all: the God who created all that the Hubble now photographs has come to be with us and to die with us and for us so that we might become holy and loving too.

Look outward, O Hubble, to the distant galaxies, but also look down and see the cross of Calvary. Oh, how we must praise God for the magnitude of his cosmic works and for the marvel of his sacrificial love!

The Hubble challenges us now to think of God differently than we ever have before because it has put so much more of his work on display. And we know that what the space telescope is seeing is only a part of the story. The rest of it involves the cross and the glory that followed it.

O Creator God, we magnify you and praise you. How can you even listen to our faltering prayers, small as we are? We believe what you have said about yourself in the Bible. We know we are precious to you. We praise you also for joining us on this speck of cosmic dust that we call the earth and for pouring out your love for our salvation. In Christ, Amen.

The Sound of Music

Speak to one another with psalms, hymns and spiritual songs.

Ephesians 5:19

How can you possibly follow this advice if you can't carry a tune in a bushel basket? Not to worry. You don't have to be able to sing well to do what the Bible describes here. But you must have the Holy Spirit.

The intriguing instruction to speak to one another with psalms, hymns, and spiritual songs follows a description of Holy Spirit fullness and contrasts it to being filled with wine. Filling yourself with wine, as some know all too well, changes behavior totally. Being filled with the Holy Spirit changes behavior totally too—for the good.

Wine will set people to singing. There is nothing surprising about the karaoke at Kilroys. Wine and song go together. Not the best songs, true, and not the best singing either, but singing does happen when the wine flows. And, says the apostle Paul, when people are full of the Holy Spirit of the living God, song happens too.

The religion of the Holy Spirit—the religion of the Bible—is a religion of singing. When the writer of Chronicles provides the tedious genealogies of God's people, he suddenly stops his ordinary description when he comes to the musicians. Heman and Asaph (1 Chron. 6:31-47), leaders of the temple musicians, step into a spotlight and their lineage is given all the way back to Israel—that is, Jacob. Clearly, among all those whose names appear in 1 Chronicles, these men are considered exceptionally important.

Indeed they are. When the apostle calls believers to "speak to one another with psalms, hymns and spiritual songs," he does so because all the great events of the Christian faith have been memorialized in song. Think of Moses and Miriam on the Red Sea shore, exulting in song as they praised God for the deliverance of the people (Ex. 15:1-21). Think of the hymns the church sang—the "mystery of godliness" hymn in 1 Timothy 3:16 and the "humbling and exalting of Christ" hymn in Philippians 2:5-11.

Think of Jehoshaphat, king of Judah, instructing the singers to go before his army into battle (2 Chron. 20:20-23). Think too of Nehemiah, who, after supervising the rebuilding of the city of Jerusalem after the exile, set up two choirs to lead the people in a rejoicing that could be heard for miles around (Neh. 12:27-43). Then, of course, there's the special praise book God gave us, complete with instructions to the musicians—the book of Psalms. The Bible is pulsating with rhythms, splendid with the music of a people who have reason to sing while in this world and who are headed for "Beulah Land," where they will sing forever (Isa. 62:4). The Bible's final book, Revelation, is full of song.

So those who have the Spirit of Christ within them will speak to each other about the great works of God that have been commemorated in song and will be celebrated throughout eternity. This does not mean the Christian life is an extended musical in which people sing to each other rather than speak, but it does mean that the subjects of the Spirit's music will be the subjects of the conversations of the redeemed.

Come now, is this realistic for us? We have so many other things we like to talk about—how we compare to Tiger Woods, where to go on our next vacation, what we found at the flea market, new ways to get rid of crab-grass. And we like to talk about the church, about preachers, So-and-so's Sunday school class, and a little whiff of scandal here and there—yes, even in the church.

True enough. But maybe, if we seldom talk about the great things of God, we need to ask God to change us. Yes, even old-timer Christians need to be converted. Paul writes in Ephesians 5 about people speaking like this because they have a melody in their hearts: "Sing and make music in your heart to the Lord, always giving thanks. . . ." Ah, yes, here is the secret— hearts renewed and overcome with astonishment because of the great work of salvation that God the Father, Son, and Holy Spirit have done for us.

O God, what do you think when you hear us speak as we do, so often for-getting to speak to one another (and about one another) in kindness and with the music of salvation? Holy Spirit, enter our hearts and revive us with the magnificent melodies of the faith. Give us a song in our hearts no matter what is happening to us. Make our speech heavenly and holy. For Jesus' sake, Amen.

Lois/Cynthia

I have been reminded of your sincere faith, which first lived in your grandmother Lois. . . .
2 Timothy 1:5

"How was your day at court?" I asked Cynthia on the phone.

"Wonderful! Ashley Grace is now my daughter."

Cynthia was jubilant; it was finally legal. When I mentioned that rearing a child these days was not the easiest thing in the world, she agreed. "But," she said, "'train up a child in the way he should go, and when he is old he will not depart from it.'"

I was happy for Cynthia, but I knew that along with her happiness there was an element of sorrow. Before three-year-old Ashley Grace became Cynthia's daughter, she was her granddaughter. Earlier, when we had talked about what Cynthia was taking on, she had said, "It's better to have a 50-year-old mother than no mother at all." Ashley is going to be in good hands.

It made me think of Lois and Eunice, who were both believers and who passed along their faith to Timothy, one of the first leaders of the Christian church. This is the ideal: when faith is passed along from grandparent to parent to grandchild. Thank God, this often happens. But sometimes it just doesn't work out that way. Sometimes it seems as if faith comes to a dead stop and won't be passed along to the next generation. That's the way it was beginning to look with Ashley Grace, until Cynthia realized what was happening and stepped in.

It's true, of course, that fifty years of age is a little old to be taking on the responsibilities of a new daughter, and Cynthia took this on with her husband's full support. But she knew and he knew that he wasn't going to be around to help for very long, sick as he was with an illness that kept the oxygen tube at his nose almost all day. He probably wouldn't see Ashley Grace's fifth birthday. Cynthia realized this, but she also realized that her granddaughter needed the attention that only she could give her. As she put it, Ashley Grace's real mother had "big-time problems."

From Lois to Eunice to Timothy, this is the way faith is supposed to travel, but nowadays parents who are themselves children of believers sometimes go through a stage in which they are no good for themselves, to say nothing of the damage they are doing to their children. Some parents are way too young when their first child is born. When you take single motherhood, divorce, and mix in a good dose of drugs and alcohol, and just plain old-fashioned laziness and indifference, you get trouble. And that's when grandparents realize that maybe their responsibilities are not entirely over, even though their nests are empty of their own children.

Nowadays the young-parent phenomenon is also yielding young grandparents, still healthy, possibly earning more money than ever. And these grandparents have developed a practical wisdom that's priceless. Like Timothy's grandmother, their faith is vital. And when they look at the needs of their children's children, they realize they have to scrap the usual model of the way grandparents are supposed to act.

Not very many will adopt their grandchildren outright, of course. Thankfully, that's not usually necessary. But people like Ashley Grace's grandmother have a great mission. If they are willing to make the sacrifices necessary to help their grandchildren, the rewards can be enormous. And, as often happens when the grandparents' faith is strong and self-sacrificial, God uses their generous helpfulness to bring correction to the very people who made the rescue necessary.

It may take years—a decade, even longer—but grandparents who are willing to help their grandchildren as Cynthia has done are often rewarded by seeing their grandchildren become children of King Jesus, and, praise God, the parents of their grandchildren often become Christ's children too. And when that happens, the chain looks like this once again: Lois—Eunice—Timothy.

Lord, look upon the shambles of broken families and show us what we must do in response. O Lord, have your people ever been persecuted as we are being persecuted, with evil forces coming right into our homes, corrupting our children? Have mercy upon us. Be with those who must take unusual action to bring rescue—people like Cynthia. Hear us for Jesus' sake, Amen.

Unmoved Movers and Shakers

Your labor in the Lord is not in vain.

I Corinthians 15:58

No matter how sad a funeral may be, it's always a thrill when you finally get to the cemetery and can read parts of 1 Corinthians 15, right there in the graveyard just before the coffin is lowered. Whenever I do it, I want to rival the trumpet of God with my shout. *My God! Praise your name! You are going to make this place a harvest field at the end of time! This is a planting we are doing here today as we bury this believer in the earth. What will she be like when you come back!? Hallelujah! Praise the Lord!*

And it's astonishing that this exciting chapter in 1 Corinthians ends with a message that puts us right back into everyday real life. Since Jesus is coming again, work hard for him today, every day. Everything you do makes a difference.

Dear brother, dear sister, it's all true that when Jesus comes back he is going to raise you with a Christlike glory-body, so don't ever let anything shake you. Don't even be shaken when the people in the white coats tell you your blood pressure is sky high or when your medical-test results are scary. Always remember there is nothing in this cursed world that can keep you from receiving the absolute fullness of Christ's salvation. Be strong as the Rock of your salvation.

Since you have this unshakable certainty, finally you can give yourself with total dedication to the work of the Lord. You can do that because you don't have a thing to worry about. Don't just stand there and do nothing now that you know you have this great future. Now you can do anything; you can go anywhere for God. The work of the Lord must now become the first priority in your life.

What is this "Lord work" anyway? Surely it's not only what preachers, missionaries, and Christian school teachers do. This is for everyone who is trusting Jesus and looking forward to spending eternity with God, wearing one of those marvelous resurrection bodies. We should think of the work of the Lord as anything and everything we do as coworkers with God as we become involved in working with God to answer the prayer Christ taught us: "Your kingdom come, your will be done on earth as it is in heaven." "Lord work" is any work that helps to make that prayer happen.

The work of the Lord is the work we do after we have begun our day in fervent prayer asking God to give us integrity, honesty, compassion, skill— whatever is needed to honor him in our divine work assignment. And nowadays it must also mean that we must boldly participate in fighting the cruel evil that contaminates this age. What about abortion? And gambling, and pornography. More work to do! What about justice in government? What about educating our children in the fear of the Lord? Oh, there is so much that needs doing. No one of us can do it all, but each of us has to find a niche and work like a glorified angel for God.

There are spiritual works too, such as the many minutes each day just spent in the presence of the triune God, praising him and praying and being molded by that overpowering book the Holy Spirit wrote.

It's astonishing that 1 Corinthians 15, so full of the excitement of Christ's victory over death, ends at my street address. And we discover that God wants us to work for him not so that we won't get bored while we wait for the trumpet to sound, but because what we do for him and in his power is not in vain. It's going to last forever. Our "Lord work" will never be destroyed.

"Lord work" is connected with glory! "Blessed are the dead who die in the Lord. . . . They will rest from their labor, for their deeds will follow them" (Rev. 14:13). "God is not unjust; he will not forget your work" of faith (Heb. 6:10). "Congratulations," he says, "you did good work—I am going to make you the ruler of many cities" (see Luke 19:17-19). Again and again the Bible says that what we do here for Christ will affect what happens to us in glory. We are saved by Jesus' blood, not by our works, but when we are saved by his blood, we have a wonderful future!

Thank you, O God, for making Christianity such an exciting, fulfilling religion. Yes, it's good to know that these wearing-out bodies of ours are going to be transformed into magnificent bodies. But, Lord, it's just as wonderful to know that our lives here are not futile; they're significant. Thank you, Jesus. Thank you, Jesus. Amen.

Meditation 81

Eye/Hand Coordination

"Throw [your right eye] away."
Matthew 5:29

Sometimes the Bible can be very dangerous, especially when you think you understand it. A student nurse in a psychological care unit discovered that a woman she had to care for had gouged out her eye after reading Matthew 5:27-30. Jesus didn't have self-mutilation in mind here—not actually going out and doing it.

If we read this passage carefully, we find lots of puzzles. For one thing, why destroy your right eye when you still have one left? Lots of people have just one eye. Men with only a left eye remaining are fully capable of looking at a woman lustfully.

The same goes for hands—why does Jesus just mention the right hand here? You can commit sin with your left one too. Of course, hands are a bit different from eyes—most people can do more with their right hand than with their left, but if their right hand is gone, many right-handed people learn to do a lot with their left.

If Jesus wanted us to take his words strictly literally here, he would have prescribed the destruction of both of our eyes and the amputation of both of our hands. He knew how eye/hand coordination is the basis of many skills, and if you have neither, there are many sins you would never be able to commit.

There is much here that is puzzling, it's true, but there is also much here that we understand perfectly well. It would be foolish for us to discard the entire passage because we have discovered some elements of it that can't be literally true. Rather, we have to let Jesus' statement here stun us and change us even more than we would be changed if we didn't have eyes and hands anymore.

Surely these words stunned the Pharisees and teachers of the law when they first heard them. They had managed to create an elaborate system of laws that they figured they largely kept. They knew the law against adultery and, thank heaven, they did not commit it. But Jesus intruded into their smugness and explained that they had it wrong. The look—yes, the look— is "heart-adultery."

If the punishment of adulterers described in Moses' law is frightening, here is another terrifying punishment: removal of the offending eye and of the hand that longs to carry through on what the eye has seen. But this is not really punishment; it's a remedy. Jesus says that we won't go to hell if we change, but if we keep looking and lusting and longing to get our hands in play we will perish everlastingly.

We must presume that Jesus knew as much about theology as we do— indeed, infinitely more! He knew that there is salvation for the vilest sinners. He knew salvation is by grace and not by works. Yet, in his Sermon on the Mount, he calls us to be perfect as his Father in heaven is perfect (Matt. 5:48). And here he indicates that the perfection must reach to the depths of our personalities and must control the roving eye and mischievous hand. Even when we do not violate the law to the point where we could miss becoming chairman of the joint chiefs of staff, God knows, God sees, God requires that we be pure right through to our hearts, with eyes and hands that do not violate that holiness.

That Jesus spoke in this way must mean that he also provides resources to those who understand that his words mean business. We may pray for the Holy Spirit's presence and for openness to the Spirit's leading, openness so actual and vital that it will be as if our offending eyes and hands have been removed.

And Jesus' words make us call out for forgiveness once again. Our righteousness, alas, is no better than that of the Pharisees and the teachers of the law. We fail to understand that God wants his Spirit-filled people to be perfectly clean inside and out.

We hear you, Lord Jesus, and we ask you, please, to do two things. First, please forgive us for catering to our baser lusts, if not with overt action then with covert glances. And help us to respond fully to your Spirit's presence within us. Overcome our tendency to commit base sin in ways that are acceptable in our society but not acceptable to you. O Christ, we are so ashamed. Amen.

The Smashing Rock

"A rock was cut out, but not by human hands."
Daniel 2:34

Why don't we read Daniel more . . . and think about it? When I read it, it becomes my favorite book, absolutely breathtaking and glorious, but then I go on to the usual things we think about in our churches and Daniel sort of fades away. What a shame!

Daniel is a book of dreams, and it's about a reality so stirring that it's the stuff that dreams are made of. When you read it early in the morning, when the house is quiet and only the noise of a distant train reminds you that there's still a world out there, the book of Daniel transports you into the kingdom of God. You feel it in your bones that Jesus is certainly going to be totally victorious; in fact, he is already.

When Nebuchadnezzar woke from his dream, he knew that something transcendently important had happened to him. He was startled, afraid, his skin crawled, his heart pounded in his chest. But for the life of him, it seems he couldn't remember all the details. In his desperation to recall them, he did a dumb thing: he told his magicians that they had to tell him what his dream was and what it meant, or they would all die. He just had to know.

Enter Daniel. (Read Daniel 2 for what leads up to this.) His doxology is splendid, before he even tells the dream—good enough to start a service of worship with: "Praise be to the name of God for ever and ever; wisdom and power are his. . . . He gives wisdom to the wise and knowledge to the discerning. . . . I thank and praise you, O God of my fathers: You have given me wisdom and power . . ." (2:20-23). What a God!

Daniel did it—he told the dream and its meaning. The king had dreamed about a big image, dazzling with its head of gold, shoulders and arms of silver, belly of bronze, legs of iron, and feet of iron and clay. As Daniel spoke, the monarch's eyes widened. Ah yes, it all came back to him. He trembled. And then, then, Daniel bent forward and said, "And while you were watching all this, your majesty, you saw a stone cut from a mountain *without human hands*. And it smashed the statue. It destroyed it all. All of it. The gold, the silver, the iron, the clay—all of it became like chaff in the wind, and that little rock became a mountain that reached up to the sky and filled the whole earth."

Not hard to figure out, your majesty; not hard to figure out for us who live today. Nebuchadnezzar could find scant encouragement in the fact that he was the head of gold, for the head and all of the rest of the image became chaff in the wind. He could only marvel and worship when he heard the denouement: "The God of heaven will set up a kingdom that will never be destroyed, nor will it be left to another people. It will crush all those kingdoms and bring them to an end, but it will itself endure forever" (2:44).

The rock, cut from the mountain without human hands—who is he, pray tell? We know who he is—Jesus Christ of Nazareth, the second person of the holy Trinity, in the flesh. He came into this world through a miracle that did not originate in human will or action. Conceived by the Holy Spirit, virgin born, God arrived on the scene, a mere stone that appeared as nothing compared to the gold and silver and bronze of the kingdoms of this world.

But this stone is God's smashing stone. All the kingdoms of the earth will fall before it, and the kingdom of God will surely be established. We must gasp with delight as we observe this great work of God. And what did the splendid monarch do? "King Nebuchadnezzar fell prostrate before Daniel and paid him honor and ordered that an offering and incense be presented to him." Would you believe it? And then he said: "Surely your God is the God of gods and the Lord of kings and a revealer of mysteries . . ." (2:46-47).

Yes, the prophecy of Daniel is a book of dreams that increase in wonder and power as the book progresses. As it turns out, they are the dreams God has for this world and for his blessed people. Here are divine dreams that have become reality through Jesus Christ, and those that are yet to be will surely come to pass.

Almighty God, we join Daniel today in praising you because you are in total control of every event happening in our world and you are establishing your glorious kingdom. Please encourage us with the assurance that your kingdom is forever, and don't let us build kingdoms to compete with yours. Help us live under your rule always. In Christ, Amen.

More than a Donkey Driver

Joseph . . . did what the angel of the Lord had commanded. . . .
Matthew 1:24

Joseph was as much the father of Jesus as Mary was Jesus' mother.

Of all people in Advent history, Joseph is most frequently shunted off to the side. Of course, we realize Mary needed him, if for nothing else but to guide the donkey from Nazareth to Bethlehem. But he was more than a donkey driver.

The fact that Joseph was as important as Mary is supported by the way the Bible treats both of them. When the angel appeared to Mary, she was confused by his announcement that she, a virgin, would have a child. After she received answers to her questions, she declared that she would most certainly do the will of God. When the angelic message came to Joseph in a dream, he was in a state of consternation because of Mary's pregnancy—he too had unsettling questions. When those questions were answered and the holy mission of Jesus was explained to him, he obeyed God just as Mary did.

Joseph is important because he established Jesus of Nazareth as the Son of David. The Messiah of Israel had to be the Son of David. We have no explicit statement that Mary was of Davidic ancestry; possibly she was a Levite like her cousin Elizabeth, John the Baptist's mother. But whatever she was doesn't really make any difference. What's important is that Jesus' earthly father was of David's tribe. And it is Joseph's Davidic ancestry that dominates the Advent story in the gospel of Matthew. The angel of the Lord addresses him as "son of David," and it is his Davidic genealogy that opens the book of Matthew. The fact that Joseph was of the house and lineage of David was what made it necessary for him and his betrothed wife to travel to Bethlehem, where the prophets had announced that Jesus would be born.

Joseph was Jesus' adoptive father—that's why he was as much Jesus' father as Mary was Jesus' mother. Anyone who would object and suggest that adoptive fathers are not as fully fathers as biological fathers would have many adoptive fathers to contend with. Fatherhood and motherhood are not first of all procreative concepts—they are moral, ethical concepts.

When Joseph agreed to take Mary as his wife, with her problem pregnancy, he gave Jesus his legitimacy among the people. Jesus could never have entered the temple if he had been illegitimate; he could never have become a rabbi.

Joseph also contributed to Jesus' humanity. It was common in those days that rabbis would have a trade, and Joseph made a carpenter out of his son. Later, when people scratched their heads in wonderment and tried to figure out who this miracle worker was, they asked, "Isn't this the carpenter?" On other occasions they asked, "Isn't this the carpenter's son?" Jesus knew how to take the measure of a wall and judge the soundness of a foundation. He had learned his trade well as Joseph's apprentice, and when he built a cabinet, it was perfect. How could it have been otherwise?

The ancient creeds declare that Jesus received his human nature from the blessed Virgin Mary. True. But his humanity became complete in the company of his earthly father. The full fatherhood of Joseph is presupposed in the Scriptures. Mary did not *believe* in the virgin birth; for her it was not an item of belief but a reality. Yet even Mary recognized Joseph as Jesus' father: "Your father and I have been anxiously searching for you," she said to the holy twelve-year-old in the temple (Luke 2:48). And we know Jesus was obedient to Joseph.

The reason we so often neglect Joseph is that we too often think of fatherhood and motherhood in terms of procreation; the biblical view is different: a father gives a person legitimacy and place in society. In Jesus' case, Joseph did all that for him.

Jesus Christ is the Son of David. Whenever we say that, we are not talking about Mary, we are talking about Joseph, who was more than a donkey driver. He was Jesus' adoptive father, and adoptive fathers are real fathers—believe me.

Lord Jesus Christ, it is so good for us to think about the fullness of your humanity. As we have thought about your adoptive father today, use our reflections to encourage those of us who are fathers to be the best we can be for our children. May many discover anew the biblical view of what fatherhood really is. In your name, we pray, Amen.

Hope and Suffering

Suffering produces . . . hope.
Romans 5:3-4

Suffering is very inconsiderate. Most of us can handle some of it; in fact, having some suffering makes you feel like one of the crowd because everybody's got some of it. In moderate amounts, suffering can be a conversation piece—but, sorry to say, full-blown suffering doesn't come that way.

A young person may discover that when you get terribly sick or chronically ill, you not only have to deal with the illness but your girlfriend or boyfriend leaves you too. Middle-aged people who deal with long-term suffering can have trouble making payments, lose their jobs, and have their high school daughter leave home at the same time. Elderly persons have themselves, their children, and their grandchildren to worry about, and sometimes there's trouble with all of them. What does an old man do, for example, when his wife's memory loss gets to the point where she doesn't recognize him? What does he do when his wife wants to go home to her mother and her mother's been dead for twenty years?

If you are suffering now, read Romans 5. Either the opening words of this chapter will send you off into gales of hysterical laughter or they will settle you down. They tell us that suffering has its good side.

Romans 5 describes suffering as a road leading to a hope that you cannot experience unless you walk the *via dolorosa*. The path looks like this: suffering yields perseverance, which yields character, which yields hope. You cannot possess a full sense of Christian hope unless you move along this path. As long as you are holding on to anything else besides God, you aren't going to experience it, but when the time comes and you see that everything is unworthy of trust and you flee to God, this other-worldly reality called the *hope of glory* suddenly bursts upon your consciousness.

Why is it necessary to be stripped of every other trust before we feel the full impact of the hope of glory? When you read Romans 5, you get the impression that so long as we are trusting in anything else besides God, we fail to fully appreciate the salvation he provides us. The apostle Paul has just finished talking about a subject that is exceedingly important for us, but, in all candor, we don't think about it all that much. In the chapter before this one he writes about justification by faith. There are whole days in which I can be busy with scores of tasks and never once give the slightest thought to my need for justification. And here the apostle talks about the possibility of rejoicing in suffering because the overriding reality that affects us is the blessed assurance that we have been justified through the righteousness of Christ.

When you really don't think you are very lost, you seldom think about the incredible mercy God has revealed in the life, death, and resurrection of Christ. You sort of figure that the whole matter of saving people is something God understands better than we do and that he will have to take care of it. Meanwhile, we expect our lives to go smoothly and we trust in lots of other things and people besides God.

Romans 5 begins by savoring the blessed truth that we have been justified by faith in Christ. And once a person realizes the truth and the impact of justification, everything else takes care of itself. We have peace with God— and what more could anyone ever want? In this situation, suffering becomes a good thing because it can peel away all our reliance on earthly things and fling us—body and soul—onto God. And once we are totally, unquestionably, solely trusting in God, we are transported to a new experience of faith; we experience the reality of hope that will never disappoint us.

When we believers read about the goodness ascribed to suffering because it leads to the hope of glory, we should not assume that we have experienced this hope fully in our lives. Paul is talking about something absolute here. This is more than the certainty of expecting to go to heaven when we die. The hope of glory is a powerful interior presence that enables the most stricken and humbled person—one who has nothing but God, and thus everything—to rejoice.

Lord, dare I ask for this presence in my life? What will it take to bring me to the point where I trust you and you only? Lord, nothing in this world can support my fragile life. Everywhere I turn, I see false saviors that I am inclined to trust. Forgive me my foolish reliance on anyone and anything besides you, my God. Fill my heart with rejoicing. In Jesus' name, Amen.

Meditation 85

How Important We Are!

We must all appear before the judgment seat. . . .
2 Corinthians 5:10

It's hard to escape the conclusion that we are unimportant. All the talk we hear about self-esteem sounds like a vehement declaration of something we know isn't really true. Getting up every morning and saying "I am somebody" just doesn't cut it—it can give us a psychological boost, but deep inside, every individual knows that he or she is just one of billions of people.

On those rare occasions when we are totally honest with ourselves, we have to admit that we really don't amount to very much. Of course, there are lots of things people can do to impress others with their importance. If they are lucky, they might become the CEO of a multibillion-dollar corporation and have their own jet. But at the end of the day, everyone's the same: just a little blip on the cosmic radar screen—here today, gone tomorrow. Teenagers knock themselves out trying to escape this bleak conclusion, and sometimes when they fail, they live recklessly and succeed in destroying themselves. But young and old all share the same problem: How do you cope with the seemingly inevitable conclusion that you really have no significance whatsoever?

Enter Jesus. He says to each one of us, "One of these days, I want to see you in front of my judgment seat, and I am going to take a look at everything you have ever done. I am going to review every thought you have ever had, and I am going to talk with you about every decision you have ever made."

"How is this possible?" we say. Well, I have no idea, just as I have no idea how God made all things, how God directs all things, and how God loves me so much that he willingly died for me.

It's frightening to think about being judged by Christ. But it's even worse not to think about it. What Jesus is saying here is that I am so significant that God is going to review everything about my life. The Bible says that this is true of everyone. Everyone I meet is important, just as I am. Each one of us is a player in a drama that has eternal consequences. If the reality of judgment allows me to think of my life as important, it by no means tells me I am more important than anyone else. All of us are moving toward the judgment seat of Christ.

Those who seek to bolster self-esteem by any means other than what we find in 2 Corinthians 5:10 play psychological games. The tricks they use to make themselves feel important yield a pseudo-self-esteem that is actually neurotic. Only when we sense that every element of our lives is so significant that it will receive the judgment of Christ can we sense the marvelous dignity of being human.

True as this may be, there is something in us that tends to feel that 2 Corinthians 5:10 is too high a price to pay for self-esteem. Is it not absolutely appalling to think that Christ is going to judge everything we do?

If you take the time to read the sentences that lead up to this verse, you will notice that they stress how Jesus gives his people his Holy Spirit, who qualifies them to do much in this life that is pleasing to God. The life-goal of Spirit-filled people is to please God. They think about pleasing God all the time—and if they do not please God all the time, at least they think about it a lot. The judgment, therefore, will reveal what is good just as well as what is evil. In other words, on the day of judgment, believers will praise God for the good things he has done in and through them.

And so far as the bad we do is concerned, the very moment we see just how dreadfully evil it really is, we will see the Savior who has paid for it all. The moment we see how much we need a Savior, we will see our Savior. What more can we ask?

Oh, it's glorious to be a Christian. We are not small! We are not insignificant! Jesus Christ is interested in everything we do. Everything. And someday, we will see just what that means.

Each day, Lord Jesus, we are moving toward the day when you will judge us. Help us to remember that nothing we do is unimportant. Inspire us with your blessed Spirit that we may do good deeds. And comfort us with the assurance that on the day of judgment we will see how you have paid for our sins. In your name, Amen.

Meditation 86

The Transfer

We . . . would prefer to be . . . at home with the Lord.
2 Corinthians 5:8

When I saw Ron in the casket, I marveled at how stunningly alive he looked. He was one of those men, still a few years shy of fifty, who had died suddenly—someone had found him in his yard on a Saturday morning where he had just begun to rake leaves. He had not intended to die, and no one had expected him to . . . just then. But in a moment, in the twinkling of an eye, long before the last trumpet sounded, he was transferred from here to God's presence.

As I looked at him, well groomed and healthy looking as he lay there, his exceptional length placing his head right at the casket's edge, he looked very undead. It's not always that way, of course. With the elderly it's different, and with those who have battled disease long and hard before they succumb. When the dead really do appear to be dead, then death seems oddly appropriate. But with Ron, it was different. What had really happened to him as he had reached with his rake for a clump of leaves and never made it? Instead the startled leaves arranged themselves around him as he lay dead among them.

Reading 2 Corinthians 4:16-5:10 can help us believers who struggle to find out what happens when fellow believers like Ron die. The apostle Paul helps us here by reminding us of something we already sense, and that is this: the real you and the real me are somewhere inside our mortal bodies. Believers are often encased in bodies that are obviously wearing out while the real person, inside, continues to grow—"Though outwardly we are wasting away, yet inwardly we are being renewed day by day."

But the main point Paul makes in these sentences is that we should remind ourselves once in a while that only our mortal bodies keep us from being in the presence of Christ. Of course we must take care of our bodies, but the apostle tells us that once we get rid of them, we will be with Jesus Christ, whom we have never seen but whom we love dearly.

There are some who claim that when believers die, they will sleep until Christ comes again; these are the "soul-sleepers." We must not deny that a case can be made for the idea that Ron is out of it now, neither interacting with his wife and son nor interacting with angels either . . . nor with Christ. But if the apostle ever heard the case to be made for soul sleep, he apparently was not impressed. He describes two options: either we are "at home in the body . . . [and] away from the Lord" or we are "away from the body and at home with the Lord."

This view of what happens to believers after they die is the same as Paul expresses in Philippians 1:20: "To me, to live is Christ and to die is gain." I well remember the first time that statement struck me. My grandfather had died, a preacher man, a little bit bothersome, always telling me I should follow in his steps. I had gone to the funeral home and viewed his body, and then I walked back to my car. As soon as the door slammed shut, and I was alone in the darkness, I burst into tears and that statement burst forth in my head: for Grandpa, living had indeed been Christ, and death for him was gain. I was not so much comforted by the thought as lifted. What a splendor—to pass at the moment of death into the gain of glory!

So what had happened to Ron? There's no way we can even begin to imagine it so long as we are here, raking our leaves. To be sure, viewed from this side of Jordan, we might wonder what good could come from his "untimely" death. It would be months before his stunned widow would be able to think about anything else. His stalwart son, collapsing in anguished tears, felt only sorrow. Ron's body, seemingly so undead, appeared capable of many more hours; it seemed able to travel so many more miles. True enough. But, good friend, the blessed truth is this: now that Ron has left his body, he is with Christ.

We are eternal beings, and when we believe that Jesus Christ is the Son of God and our Savior, there is nothing, *nothing,* not even death, that can interrupt our lives. Death, in fact, only makes our lives better.

O living Savior, we thank you that we can go to the house of mourning and experience jubilation in the presence of death. Touch our mourning hearts with your Gilead balm and assure us that the life we have in Christ already will never be interrupted by anything, not even by death. Please comfort Ron's wife and son with the hope of glory. In your name, Amen.

Meditation 87

Empty Christians

Your attitude should be the same as that of Christ Jesus.

Philippians 2:5

In 1997 the Chinese noticed that in countries where there's Christmas, there's a lot of buying and selling going on, and they figured that they could use a season of the year in which that happened in their country too. So China now has Christmas—it's just another example of how widespread the Christmas holiday is. It's sad, though, that a majority of people celebrate Christmas for the wrong reasons. Yet there is no religious holiday that is celebrated by more people in more places.

Believers tend to feel uneasy about the secularized celebration of Christmas, because for them the remembrance of Christ's birth is a glorious spiritual holiday; they shudder as they see the commercialization of this day. The event at its center is so far beyond our ability to comprehend that we can only stand with the shepherds and marvel. There are words we can use to talk about what happened, but once we have said them or put them down on paper, we must admit we really don't know what we are talking about. *Christmas is about God becoming a human being.* Now, what could that possibly mean?

The apostle Paul wrote about this event in his letter to the Philippians, stressing the utter humiliation that Christ's entering our race involved. The words Paul uses in Philippians 2 are really the words of a hymn that Christians sang back then, a hymn called the *Carmen Dei.* With it, believers sought to express what happened. God, the second person of the Trinity, laid aside the glory and power of his deity and became one of us.

The Bible message is that God, who is ultimate reality, is a loving, giving God who is willing to give himself to the uttermost for the salvation of his people. No illustration can come close to helping us understand what was involved in this emptying. It's a unique act, without parallel in the universe.

Just as astonishing as the fact of God's humiliation in Jesus Christ, however, is the fact that this God now calls us to imitate what Christ has done. And we are to imitate him on the level of "attitude," or, to use another word, on the level of "mind." The infinitely loving attitude of Jesus Christ compelled him to do what he did for us, and now we who believe in him are called to have the same attitude he had.

The God who saves us is the God who emptied himself, and now we, in response to the wonder of his grace, are called to empty ourselves as well. And what did the second person of the Trinity empty himself of? He emptied himself of himself. To be sure, while he was among us, he retained his divine being, but he laid aside his divine characteristics and prerogatives. If he had not done that, the stable into which he was born would not have been able to contain him. Mary would not have been able to take him into her arms. If he had retained his divine characteristics, he would have resembled the glory of the angels who announced his birth, and everyone would have fallen back in terrified astonishment.

Now you and I must empty ourselves too. What does this mean? Of what are we to empty ourselves? Well, we are to empty ourselves of ourselves.

Once I read the testimony of a man who had been deeply moved by God and who felt compelled to serve God in his mission. In his testimony he referred to all the skills he had, all the things he learned, and all that he felt he brought to God's mission. I know the man, and I know that he meant well. But as I read his statement, I realized that he would have to learn that when we give ourselves in service to the Lord, we must begin by emptying ourselves of what we are. We have nothing to offer to our Savior, nothing at all.

At Christmas and every day, we must ask Christ to give us the same attitude he had. We cannot generate this attitude within our own hearts. How strange to ask for emptiness! But when we receive Christ's attitude, we are filled with his Holy Spirit and then, only then, can he use us.

Loving Lord Jesus, thank you for your willingness to empty yourself for us. How could this ever happen? How could you ever be contained within the body of an ordinary mortal? Please give us your Holy Spirit's power so that we may become more and more like you, deep within. Empty us of ourselves and fill us with yourself, O Christ. Amen.

Meditation 88

The Bells on the Horses

On that day HOLY TO THE LORD *will be inscribed on the bells. . . .*
Zechariah 14:20

There are brief moments in life when something strikes you with such power that you suddenly feel tears come to your eyes. Sometimes it can be a moment in which the simple statement of a little child cuts through many layers of confusion and suddenly you see something about reality you hadn't seen before.

Sometimes these moments occur during times of worship. There can be a flash of insight from a sermon, or the overwhelming power of an anthem can nearly bring you to tears. It's not often that something like this happens to us when we are out there in fast-moving traffic, trying to keep from getting killed. But some time ago it happened to me when I was passing a semi.

It was a new rounded-body tractor, either a Kenworth or a Freightliner. As I pulled abreast of the monster, there, high on its nose, just before the curve to the top of the hood, I saw the simple words "Jesus is Lord." It startled me. And then, just as suddenly, it hit me in much the same way that a high moment in worship sometimes does. "How beautiful!" I said to myself.

The placement of the statement "Jesus is Lord" and the modest lettering used to make it told me that it was not meant to communicate anything to those of us who were passing the vehicle; it was actually a confession that that truck belonged to Jesus. When I had passed the semi and pulled into the lane in front of it, I wanted somehow to let the driver know I had seen his statement and had been touched by it. But you know how it is with these big trucks—it's almost impossible to see the driver if you are in a regular car, as I was. About all you can see is the grill and the headlights and you keep hoping that the rig won't roll over you.

That simple statement on the hood of that tractor expresses the essence of the Christian faith. That truck and its driver expressed Christianity better than many of us do as we scurry about our busy work in the church and kingdom. Christ's work is so wonderfully broad that it's possible for believing truckers to dedicate their semi-tractors to Christ.

The great goal of God's work of salvation in Jesus is the restoration of all creation. Jesus did not die and rise again only to snatch disembodied souls from hell; he did it so that what God intended for this earth, for us, would finally be put in place. What he intended was that we learn that Jesus is Lord of everything we do.

One Old Testament prophet said that the day is coming when the bells on the horses in Jerusalem will be inscribed with the words "HOLY TO THE LORD." The ordinary cooking pots in the temple will be as holy as the specially sanctified utensils used for offering. Life's ordinary accouterments will be bathed in holiness. The prophet knew that the day would come when believers would announce that Jesus is Lord of their tractors and trailers as they tooled down the highway.

Once, after an especially magnificent description of God's sovereign grace sent the apostle Paul into an ecstasy of praise, he went on to say that now, because of God's mercy, we must give our entire lives as "living sacrifices" to God (Rom. 12:1). He realized that because Jesus has finished his great work of salvation and sent his Holy Spirit into the lives of his people, believers will learn the art of transforming every element of their lives into a sacrifice of gratitude that they present each day to their Savior.

They do what that trucker did. It's as if they go through their houses and write "Jesus is Lord" on all their possessions. They walk out into their garages and scrawl "Jesus is Lord" across their tools. As they work at their assigned tasks in the office or on the assembly line, they see the words "Jesus is Lord" on everything they touch and handle.

At the end of the day, they say, "Lord, I did it all for you." I think that trucker must have had something like that in mind when he wrote "Jesus is Lord" on that dusty Kenworth . . . or Freightliner . . . whatever it was.

Almighty God, we remember now that when you created all things, you wanted your lordship to be uppermost within our world. So often your lordship is forgotten and disdained. Thank you for truckers who want the world to know their truck belongs to you. May we learn from them, and may we be obedient in our lives once again today. In Christ our Lord, Amen.

Timothy, My Son

Paul . . . to Timothy my true son in the faith. . . .

I Timothy 1:2

Centuries before the apostle Paul wrote to Timothy, the prophet Isaiah had said that God would give eunuchs who hold fast to his covenant a name better than sons and daughters (Isa. 56:5). True enough, but, praise God, he also gives children like Timothy to the childless who trust him.

It would be wrong for us to sentimentalize the relationship between Paul and Timothy, though it no doubt had its warm and personal side. Paul likely shed a few tears for this young man—when he left him in Ephesus, for example, and went on. But when Paul calls Timothy his son, he is talking about the way the Christian church is put together. It is good that we understand this.

When the apostle had come to Lystra in the province of Galatia on his first missionary journey, a mother and her daughter had been converted, Lois and Eunice. These godly women immediately perceived what the apostle was doing: he was using the Old Testament Scriptures to prove that Jesus was the Christ, the Messiah, the Son of God. So Lois, the mother, and her adult daughter, Eunice, studied the Scriptures. Eunice was married to a Greek who had rejected the gospel.

Lois and Eunice also taught the Scriptures to Timothy, Eunice's son, who was still very young. In fact, Paul later reminded Timothy that he had learned the Scriptures from infancy. So when Paul returned to Lystra on his second journey to spread the gospel, believers pointed out the young man Timothy, who was a fruit of his first visit, well trained in the Old Testament Scripture by two godly women, his grandmother and his mother. The believers said to Paul: "You should take him with you." And Paul did . . . after circumcising him (for they would speak to many Jews) and ordaining him through the laying on of hands.

"Timothy my true son"—what did this mean? It meant that Timothy had received the apostolic teaching. He had received it first of all through his godly mother and grandmother, who had taught him effectively and accurately. And he had been with Paul and had heard him do it again and again: Paul would take the Scriptures and prove that Jesus was the Christ, the Son of God.

Timothy was not Paul's son in the sense that many years of travel together had created tender, human bonds between them (though that most certainly must have happened); he was his son because through Paul the divine teaching had been passed on to Timothy. Timothy's natural father, who was an unbeliever, could not do that. Paul was his real father, and Timothy was his true son.

We must learn to think about fatherhood the way the Bible presents it. We seldom do. We usually think of fatherhood in very naturalistic ways. We think of it in terms of procreation and conception. We would tend to view Paul's statement to Timothy as a figure of speech, saying, "Of course, Paul was not his true father," and we would be wrong. We might think that Paul is using the idea of *son* here in a derivative way. Not at all. Fatherhood, according to the Bible, is first of all a spiritual idea. Fathering a child on the natural level requires very little effort. But true fathering requires much; it requires faith and dedication.

To be a Christian is to have the right father. It is in fact to become a son, a daughter, of Paul, as Timothy was. Lois and Eunice were Paul's daughters. Being a Christian means finding your father—Paul, and Christ (the "Everlasting Father"—Isa. 9:6), and Christ's Father—ultimately everything goes back to Christ's Father. "Jesus," we ask, "how should we pray?" and he answers, "Say, 'Our Father in heaven. . . .'"

Blessed are those children whose natural parents bring them the teaching of God the Father. But, thanks be to God, many whose birth fathers do not have faith become true sons of Paul and of Christ, and they receive all the special gifts that come from the "Father of the heavenly lights, who does not change like shifting shadows" (James 1:17).

O Father in heaven, thank you for giving us special people who can become our true fathers while we are in this world. We thank you for fathers and mothers who believe in you and who have taught us your Word. Whatever our natural parentage, may we believe in your Son fully and receive the glorious truth that binds us to him and to you, Father of the heavenly lights. In your Son's name, Amen.

Absolutely Nothing

[Nothing] will be able to separate us from the love of God. . . .
Romans 8:39

What happens to you in your heart of hearts when God calls you to deal with multiple catastrophes?

Many of us can handle one. Somewhere inside, there are the resources that help us through. Sometimes, when something dreadful happens, believers discover to their amazement that they feel closer to God than ever. But when there are more than one, what happens to our ability to handle things? For example, let's say one tragic death follows another. You try to handle the second one, but along with handling it, it seems you relive every minute of the grief you felt when the first death occurred.

When catastrophes come in bunches, deep, unsettling questions come in bigger bunches. "This must be a nightmare," you think, and you say, "O God, please wake me up." But it's not a nightmare; it's reality. And then you wonder what God is doing to you. Where is his mercy?

Job bemoaned his plunge into misery this way: "God assails me and tears me in his anger and gnashes his teeth at me. . . . All was well with me, but he shattered me; he seized me by the neck and crushed me. He has made me his target; his archers surround me. Without pity, he pierces my kidneys and spills my gall on the ground. Again and again he bursts upon me; he rushes at me like a warrior" (Job 16:9-14).

Often when we are smitten with one sorrow after another, we regress and become like Job. We forget—the calamities cloud our poor minds, and we cannot remember Romans 8. That's when our friends must come to us and lay their hands on our arm and tenderly remind us of the love of God.

In this magnificent chapter the apostle Paul, who dealt with calamity a time or two, emphasizes that no matter what happens to us at any time, God's love is still with us, in our lives. He says, "I am convinced that neither death nor life, neither angels nor demons, neither the present nor the future, nor any powers, neither height nor depth, nor anything else in all creation, will be able to separate us from the love of God that is in Christ Jesus our Lord."

I am thinking of a woman who lost her husband in a helicopter crash—thirty-nine years old, out there working his territory, supporting his family, trying to make a go of it . . . and dead! Later her son was murdered at age thirty-eight—a missionary brutally gunned down in Ecuador before the very eyes of his wife and little children. How do the words of the apostle strike her? I can only pray that they will pierce the fog of paralyzing grief.

Where was God in all this? Couldn't he have arranged another flight for her husband? Can't he even protect his own missionaries? These ugly, nagging questions batter believers and make them ashamed.

Being a believer does not make one immune to Job-like questions, but being a believer does allow for Paul's convictions to find their way into our own lives. Paul moves far beyond Job. He catalogs every conceivable reality that might possibly separate us from God's love—not angels and demons, not even death itself, no, nothing observable or imaginable can put those who trust in Christ outside of God's loving care. And Paul can do this because God has made it possible in Christ and through his Holy Spirit.

The cross and the resurrection show us that God's love in Christ is the supreme reality in the universe. God wants his people to know that even in their "deepest hell" he loves them.

We are vulnerable on so many levels and in so many ways. Every heartbeat, every breath, every function of our bodies has its danger side. Human relationships can be crushing. The people we love are in danger too, and we are in danger with them. Things happen. Stuff happens. And sometimes you feel you will weep forever.

But the love of God is there, in it all, through it all. And those who believe that God's very own Son died for them really do believe God loves them. But sometimes it's so hard. So hard. . . .

Loving God, we know that you know what we go through every day. Help us each moment to turn our eyes on Christ, and, remembering his cross, may we believe that it's true: nothing ever can separate us from your love. Holy Spirit, help us to believe this. Overcome our desperate doubts. Help us to trust you fully. Through Christ, Amen.

Wholehearted Devotion

His heart was not fully devoted to the LORD his God.

I Kings 11:4

We are often told to read the Bible for inspiration, but the truth is that there are long stretches of this book that leave us depressed. The history of the nations of Judah and Israel, which occupy so many pages of the sacred text, often fills us with consternation. Take the history of Solomon, for example.

Few men have been more blessed than this man—his wisdom and knowledge were so world-renowned that kings and at least one queen came from far away to hear him. But he had heart trouble. His heart was not fully devoted to God. He was not loyal to God as his father, King David, had been.

No, reading about Solomon is not inspirational, but it is useful to know about him and about his downfall. He was a modern man—he was like us who live today. For one thing, he was captivated by sensuality—he loved his harem, and the women in it led him to worship false gods.

If you analyze what happened to God's special people in the Old Testament era, it wasn't that they completely turned their back on the true God who had revealed himself to them. God had actually appeared to Solomon twice and had warned him about idols, but Solomon wanted to have it all: the worship of the true God and the fun that went along with idolatry. His religion turned out to be a weird, disastrous mixture: "Solomon showed his love for the LORD by walking according to the statutes of his father David, except that he offered sacrifices and burned incense on the high places" (1 Kings 3:3).

We who worship the true God who has come to us in Jesus Christ make a dreadful mistake if we read material like this and assume that we are not like Solomon. If Solomon, who benefited from direct appearances from God and who received special gifts from God, stumbled, who are we to think we are not capable of doing the same?

We must never forget that our faith is a matter of the heart. We cannot worship God as we should unless we have a perfect heart, a loyal heart, a heart that is wholly devoted to the true God.

Jesus was getting at this when he said that no man can serve two masters and when he said that we cannot serve God and money (Matt. 6:24). Do you know any Christians who are trying to serve God and money? Come now, they are as plentiful as mosquitoes in summertime. And money, of course, is not just something measured in dollars and cents, but it's a powerful force that provides security and clout.

And Solomon's sensuality—how many who claim to know Christ also want their sensual enjoyment? If necessary, they are willing to chuck a couple of the commandments to get it.

Idolatry still abounds. Perceptive readers of the Scriptures and of our times would be able to show you that the old idolatry has never disappeared; it is here now more than ever, but the idols are disguised. What is it but the worship of false gods that compels people to destroy their children?

No, the entire Bible is not inspirational; some of it is downright disgusting. But those parts are there to jerk our chain and wake us up and shatter our naiveté. I must be sure that I do not think of my worship of the true God primarily in terms of what happens in church on Sunday. I must always be alert to the presence of idols and set a guard around my eyes and control my hands and direct my mind in such a way that I do not end up worshiping the false gods of this age.

It took about seven hundred wives and three hundred concubines to lead Solomon's heart away from God. But for us all it takes is some late-night television or a ramble through the smut sites on the Internet. If you read the whole Bible and think about its total message, you can never say you haven't been warned. Inspired? Not always. But there are some things we need as much as we need inspiration. Like knowledge. Like warning.

Almighty God, make us diligent in our use of your Holy Word so that its message may make us wise and strong. Open our eyes so that we will be able to discern the idolatry that abounds around us. Make us alert to our own tendencies to divide our hearts, our loyalties. Through your Holy Spirit enable us to give you our wholehearted devotion. In Christ we pray, Amen.

Meditation 92

Satisfied

My soul will be satisfied. . . .
Psalm 63:5

Few psalms surpass Psalm 63 in its expression of nearly sensuous love for God. A high point in the psalm is the sentence translated in the New International Version as "My soul will be satisfied as with the richest of foods. . . ." Here is a case in which a translation does its best but misses the sheer ecstasy that the writer meant to convey.

Since souls don't eat, they can hardly be satisfied with anything that comes from the supermarket. The supermarket is not in the picture here; a more primitive feast is. The animal has been slaughtered, young and tender, roasted over the spit; now it is time to eat, and those who are around the table go for the choicest viands, savoring each rich, juicy morsel. And they lean back and grin, as a warm glow of comfortable fullness overspreads them. It is so-o-o-o . . . GOOD!

There's a curious intermingling of the spiritual and the physical in this wondrous psalm of human/divine encounter. David (let us associate this psalm with him, as the Bible does) begins by ascribing frantic thirst to his soul and parched longing to his body as he speaks of his intense desire for God. We who restrict our religious expressions to certain set times and places and who are astonished when occasionally we find ourselves overcome with spiritual fervor must understand that when we read Psalm 63, we are in another country. Here worship does not begin at 10:30 on a Sunday morning and run for an hour till coffeetime. Here the worshiper and God are locked in an embrace that makes time stand still and all other reality fall away.

What is it precisely that makes David so ecstatic? It's the love of God, his lovingkindness, his tender mercy. God's ultimate attribute, sometimes obscured in the Scriptures by his wrath and jealousy, especially in the older testament, has always been on display for those who earnestly have pursued their search for him. For such passionate seekers now, this love clicks into focus whenever they call to mind the cross of God's dear Son. "Lift high the cross"—no, reach high and grasp it and then embrace it and know that the flesh of Jesus has been torn and the blood of Jesus has been poured out for the complete remission of all your sins. Sit back, smile, and feel the glow from head to toe. My soul is satisfied just as my body is satisfied by a delicious, overflowing banquet table.

Before we become too jealous of David's high emotion, we should notice that it is written by a fugitive in the desert, and with that in mind we should receive its instruction, which is not entirely welcome. Psalm 63 is yet another of the Bible's revelations of a fundamental spiritual equation. It goes like this: *Physical and Emotional Hardship often becomes the occasion for Spiritual Renewal and Fulfillment.* We might write that PEH=SRF. David here is in desert flight before his tormentors. Their lies have destroyed his reputation, and their sword is eager to taste his blood. He is physically drained and emotionally distraught; in that condition he experiences the fullness of life on the deepest level of experience. He senses God's saving presence and gratefully receives his love and help.

"I sing beneath the shadow of your wings," he cries. "I stay close to you; your right hand upholds me."

Yesterday, before writing this, I read this psalm with a woman who has been bed-ridden for eight years with MS. "Nothing works anymore," she said. And then she added, smiling, "And I am content." I heard a preacher read this psalm once, chemo-bald from a deadly cancer, with his wife only two weeks from cancer death; he had learned the wonder of its message.

We learn the wonder of this psalm in our extremity. Desert fugitives who know the blessed Savior understand. When we look at our lives very closely, we see there is much desert in them too.

Oh, to be satisfied with the love of God!

Loving God, help us to be dissatisfied with the usual carefully controlled moments for worship we have programmed into our lives. Give us the holy yearning for the deep experience of your lovingkindness. Make us aware that our usual shelters are fragile and will fail us. Let us sing in the shadow of your wings. Through the loving Christ, Amen.

Tattooed Tears

"God will wipe every tear from their eyes."
Revelation 7:17

Tears come early and stay late. Children can switch from laughter to tears in an instant. Sometimes they cry because terrible things happen to them. Some children cry because they are famished and there's no food in sight. We adults cry a lot too; sometimes the tears break over the retaining wall of convention and pour like a torrent down our cheeks. Someday, the Bible says, tears will be obsolete for God's people.

The other day I met a young man who had a permanent tear; I wonder if it will ever be wiped away. Right at the corner of his eye, on his upper cheek, there's a tattooed tear you see as soon as you look at him. Will God be able to wipe it away too? It's a real tattoo, and real ones don't come off. It's a poor job, done by someone who wasn't too good at tattooing, and the skin is soft there around the eye. Looks to be there permanently.

I met the young man one Sunday morning as a service we held in the prison drew to a close. The men who attended the service had heard again that there is salvation for the lowliest of people, the vilest of sinners, and they had lined up so that some of us who were there, volunteer counselors at that point, could hear their needs and pray with them. After it was about all over, this young man walked over to me.

He was short and slight, with his hair tightly braided, close to his scalp. I had noticed him in some of the sessions we had had the day before, and he seemed small and helpless. As I bent near to hear his voice, he told me that he believed in Jesus as his Savior, but, please, would I pray that he would become more like Christ? He needed more strength to fight sin. I put my arm around his shoulder and we huddled together at Jesus' cross. What will become of that poor man with his tattooed tear?

Nothing macho here. How long can a man be macho nowadays? There are so many things to weep about. When a group of prisoners in a meeting of about a hundred men were asked how many had children, most of their hands went up, and they all knew they were neglecting their kids. They were far from their children and from their wives, or their wives had simply given up on them. Today the twisted agony of human relationships brings tears. It's hard to be macho.

Then too there are the endless defeats that so many people who seem to be losers experience day after day. "Hey, brother, why you got that tear?" People would ask him that, I suppose, and he might say, "Just look at me: I'm small, I don' amount to nothin', and I got seven more years on this stretch ahead of me. And when I walk outta here, how do I know I'll be strong enough to keep from comin' right back in?" It's hard to be macho. Might as well be honest and say to Janey with her needle: "Hey, Janey, just put a tear right there at the corner of my eye, 'cause my tears ain't never goin' away."

It's hard to be macho these days—there's so much gut-wrenching sorrow. You feel it in a prison in a special way, but a prison is really nothing more than a concentrated version of what is going on outside. Outside, the pain and misery are more spread out, and there are no walls or guard towers or razor wire. People build their own prisons for themselves outside; drugs can become prison walls; anger and bitterness and failure can become prison walls too. It's hard to be macho.

The gospel message is this: "Don't have to be." All we need to do is turn to Christ and surrender to him totally. He begins wiping our tears already in this world; and he will finish the job when we are in glory. Even tattooed tears can come off when Christ's finger touches the eyes of little people who figure failure is their middle name.

So the young prisoner and I clung to each other for a few brief moments, he with his permanent tear on his cheek and I with my tears more carefully concealed. But in those brief moments we both believed it: God will wipe these tears away. Now the trick is to live each moment with the joy that Christ has come to give us.

O tender Jesus, touch us with your tear-removing power. For me and for all people tears are a permanent fixture of life. Thank you for the assurance that the day will come when those who trust in you will have no reason to cry anymore. O Christ, we know you have made this possible because while you were here, you wept more than any of us ever will. Thank you. In your name, Amen.

Meditation 94

Dirty Old Men

The older ones [went] first. . . .
John 8:9

The stunning vignette of the woman caught in adultery has managed to remain in many Bibles, though most Bible scholars agree that it was not in the original manuscript. But it attached itself to the sacred text early and has not been dislodged because it's alive with marks of authenticity. This event most likely actually occurred, and there is so much here worth mulling over—little details that startle us and set us pondering.

What we have here is a drama alive with primitive power: a woman caught in *flagrante delicto* was hauled unceremoniously before Jesus. It's likely that those who brought her considered their confronting Christ with this corrupted lady as a stern reprimand, for he was known to spend time with people of stained reputation. It was as if they said, "Now there, see such a person, fresh from her assignation, without a nanosecond to repent—how do you react to *her*?"

There is sex here, raw and compelling, and there is much of such sex in the Bible. I think of Phinehas, described in Numbers 25, who centuries earlier thrust his sword through two people whom he caught just as this woman had been caught; Cozbi was the woman who was killed back then. Judah, Jesus' distant forebear, had his trouble with sex. And for that matter so did David, the king of Israel. No wonder it still causes so much misery.

The writer of this tense episode provides us with precise details. The excited accusations of the woman's tormenters are here, the quietness of Jesus as he stooped down to write the only words we know of that he ever wrote, and then his simple response to the suggestion that the woman be stoned as Moses' law demanded: "If any one of you is without sin, let him be the first to throw a stone at her."

There could have been bloodshed and death here. Read Moses' law book, and you will see that it demands stoning. Adultery is evil, let there be no question about that. But there are sins that are worse, or at least just as bad—like self-righteous vindictiveness. In some strange way, Jesus' demeanor, or possibly what he wrote, which some of them craned their necks to see and then whispered along down the line—whatever it was, suddenly there was a brilliant flash of moral vision. They saw themselves and understood their own sin. How long their realization of sinfulness lasted we do not know, but just then it took them by the throat and stopped their words. They stood silent. And they left.

The woman's accusers left, beginning with the dirty old men. It was as if the realization of their own sin touched each one separately. It took some longer than others to catch on. They left "one at a time," the Bible says. And the full meaning of what Jesus had conveyed hit the older ones first. They were the first to leave.

It's interesting that when you read the original Greek text, you read that it was the *presbyters* who left first. What did these older men sense? What did they see?

Could it have been that they suddenly realized just how wretched their conduct was? Did they sense that they had had their own cheap thrill from finding this woman in her compromising circumstance and dragging her rudely to the Lord? (And where, pray tell, was the woman's companion?) Did Jesus' response strip away the facade of moral superiority so that they suddenly saw they were not much different from the woman they accused?

Or did their age suddenly allow them to see what was happening from the perspective of their years? Did they suddenly remember embarrassing incidents in their own pasts and see the depth of their hypocrisy?

Who can say? But we are left to ponder this brief episode. There is something here for all of us. And old men will wonder especially. And deep in their hearts they will know why men their age were the first to leave.

Lord Jesus, help us use what we read in John 8 to see the folly of our censorious attitudes and actions. Through your Holy Spirit, do not let us dwell on the sins of others, but rather enable us to see the sins we are guilty of. Thank you, O Christ, for dying on the cross to make forgiveness possible even for us old sinners. In your name, Amen.

Forgiven Sinners

Blessed is he whose transgressions are forgiven. . . .
Psalm 32:1

Earlier I mentioned that 2 Samuel 11 is one of two Bible chapters that trouble me the most; the other one is Genesis 3. That chapter in Genesis is about our race's fall into sin—if it were not true, we wouldn't have war and tears and IVs and caskets. The chapter in 2 Samuel is about David's unspeakable double sin—make that triple: covetousness, adultery, murder.

But when God enters the picture, beautiful things happen. When God finally took hold of David and broke down his stubborn denial, David confessed everything and received God's gracious forgiveness. More than likely the psalm we are looking at was pressed from his broken heart. He saw that the forgiveness of God is the most precious gift in the world.

We all need it. You realize that when you recognize what sin actually is and you see how much there is in your own life.

Think of David and Bathsheba—why did he do what he did? On the one hand, the answer is easy. We are sexual creatures, and sex starts early and stays late. But it wasn't just the sex here, it was the treachery—making sure the woman's husband was killed in battle. Captain Uriah, good soldier that he was—decorated, disciplined, dedicated, and run through with an enemy's sword outside Rabbah's walls. David, how could you do that?

Answer: He could do it because he could do it. Sin is a matter of doing what we are able to do with no reference to God. He did it because he was king. He could do what he wanted to do. If he saw a woman he wanted, he could have her. He was king. If it meant eliminating her husband, he could do so. He was king. In those days husbands with beautiful wives did well not to let kings see their wives. David could do what he wanted. No one would stop him.

This is what our sin is too. With David, the sin was especially reprehensible, but that is not always the case. Whenever we do as we please without any reference to God, we sin against him. Someone asked me once, "What does the Bible mean when it says, 'Everything that does not come from faith is sin'?" (Rom. 14:23). Well, figure it out. If we do what we want to do, with no reference to God, then what we are doing is sin.

The Spirit-controlled life is one that always assesses responsibility to God and to our neighbor. To be sure, it can become pretty tedious having to ask God whether we should buy real ice cream or a fat-free substitute or whether we should play tennis this afternoon or visit Joseph in the hospital. Tedious, yes, but somehow faith and understanding God's will is involved in all this decision making. Should I build a new house? Should I buy a new car? Should I buy a luxury car? Should I expand my business? Should I switch jobs? Should I flirt with that cute gal at the office—just flirt, of course? Should I give more money to the church? Should I spend more time reading? Reading the Bible? Should I quit school and go to work? Let's just say that you could do any one of these things fairly easily; no one would really criticize you. You are enough of a king to have options like these. Well, sin is doing what we want without ever asking what God wants of us.

And when we act as if sin is a problem that other people have, we get sick, as David did—our bones waste away and we end up groaning all day long (Ps. 32:3). We end up gaining the whole world and losing our own soul. And then, one day, we see just how far away we are from God, just how miserably self-centered we are. Maybe we have not arranged to have anybody killed, but that could well be because we really don't have it in our power to make arrangements like that. If I were king like David, would I do it then?

I carry the label *sinner* stamped across my person like a USDA mark on a side of beef. Praise God that he is merciful and forgives sin and that he makes sinners like me blessed people through Jesus, who took David's sins on himself, and my sins too—and yours, if you trust Jesus for your salvation.

Oh, how we thank you, God of all grace, that you forgive sinners like us. Forgive us for the sin of blindness that keeps us from seeing that we sin against you so often. Lord, we frequently act like kings who can do as they please. And often we actually do as we please. Enter us with your power and change us and bless us with your forgiveness. For Jesus' sake, Amen.

The Purpose of Sickness

"This sickness . . . is for God's glory. . . ."
John 11:4

One of the most exasperating times for a family occurs when all get sick together. When everyone has to use the bathroom at once, an ordinarily calm household can become pretty wild.

Such episodes evoke wry smiles when they are over. But when serious, life-threatening, even terminal, disease strikes more than one member of a family at once, all of us are stunned. When a husband and wife who have been healthy become victims of the same cruel enemy at the same time, we are shocked and confused. Surely God should arrange things better than that. When two people in the same household are facing death together, we cringe and roll our eyes heavenward and ask, "Why, Lord?"

When we find ourselves wondering what God is up to as hideous illness intrudes, it's good to read John 9 and 11. In John 9, we find Jesus' disciples reacting to a man who had always been blind. While his disability was chronic, their question and Jesus' answer can help even when we think of illness that strikes suddenly and brings death soon after.

The disciples, as was customary in those days, automatically connected serious illness with sin. In the case of the man born blind, establishing such a connection was complicated by the fact that his disability was a birth defect. Though it was preposterous to connect the man's illness with his own culpability, the disciples were, apparently, willing to consider the possibility of the unborn sinning. In fact, their query is viewed by some as evidence that the idea of prenatal sin was fairly common then. This illustrates how far people will go in trying to find a reason for sickness.

Jesus rejected this curious notion and also the idea that the blind man's parents may have been implicated. Instead he startled his disciples and us still today with the announcement that this man's disability was to be an occasion for the display of God's work. There seems to be every justification for us to apply to this episode the very statement Jesus made later, in John 11, when he said that the death of his friend Lazarus would result in God being glorified by providing Jesus with an occasion to display his power.

It requires great faith for us to transfer all this to our own critical circumstances. How can we even consider this possibility when, as Job put it, that which we feared has happened to us? Yet we must pray in times of terrifying extremity that we will be given the grace to sense that a divine advantage will most certainly be achieved through our trials.

It is strangely true that when believers are tried, they pass beyond their usual experience of faith to a mystical experience of God's presence. When things are going well in our lives, the tranquillity is a barrier to experiencing our dependence upon God fully. But when our vulnerability is revealed and we see the full extent of our dependence on God for every heartbeat and every mysterious process that occurs in our bodies, we sense how close he is to us each moment. Everything takes on new meaning. We enter into a new level of communion with God and a new level of trust in him.

Jesus' healing of the man born blind led to a pivotal confrontation with the Jewish religious establishment; Jesus' raising of Lazarus from the dead precipitated the week-long final confrontation that ended at Calvary. In both cases, the supremacy of Christ was displayed and God was glorified.

Believers are well aware that there are statements in Scripture that assure them that all things that happen to them are for their good. It is one thing to know this with your head; it is another thing to know it from personal experience. Among believers, there is a precious band of those who are dying and who know it and who are absolutely certain that God will do his work with them and will glorify himself in their lives. With victorious joy they declare, "For me, to live is Christ and to die is gain" (Phil. 1:21). From them we learn what we could learn nowhere else.

Almighty and loving God, we submit to you. Some who read this are at the place of mighty dread. Others of us are waiting for the trial to begin. Whatever our circumstances, help us believe, help us believe, that you will glorify yourself in our lives. Help us sense our privilege as we suffer. In Christ, our Lord, Amen.

Meditation 97

Seeing Jesus

We shall be like him. . . .
I John 3:2

The greatest frustration of being a Christian is that everything about our faith centers on a person we have never seen. Thankfully, our faith is supported by documents that have been written by people who were eye-witnesses to Christ's glory.

The apostle who wrote the sentence we are looking at now was one of those eyewitnesses. He opens his brief letter to the churches by reminding them that he actually saw the eternal Christ and touched him. This means that when we read John's gospel, the other gospels, and this letter to the churches, we are only one step removed from actually seeing Christ ourselves. Even so, the fact remains that we have not yet done so.

The apostle Peter, who was with John at the transfiguration, seemed to sense how difficult it is for believers like us to follow Christ, having never seen him. He acknowledges this problem when he describes Christ as the one whom we love, though we have never seen him (1 Pet. 1:8).

But the day will come when we will see Jesus, and John's letter tells us that when we see him, the transformation will occur that Paul envisioned in Romans 8. There Paul said that we have been "predestined to be conformed to the likeness of [God's] Son, that he might be the firstborn among many brothers" (8:29). The fullness of this transformation, or conformation, will be accomplished when we see Jesus in glory.

The fact that we do not talk more about looking forward to seeing Jesus is probably due to our failure to read the Bible more. Or, if we do read it a lot, we tend to slide by its description of what seeing Jesus will be like. But this possibility should be a dominant element of our anticipation as we look ahead into the future. Often people will talk about the fact that they are looking forward to seeing a loved one, possibly an infant whom they buried before the dear child could ever act or react. But few of us get a sparkle in our eyes when we think about how glorious it will be to see the person who is the center of our faith, Jesus Christ.

John tells us that when we finally see Jesus, our current status as "God's children" will reach its fullest degree. The apostle Paul also speaks about what it means to be a child of God who calls the Almighty "Daddy" and then carries this forward to the ultimate conformation to Christ's very likeness. So, John too says that when we see Christ, we will be like him.

It's impossible for us to understand how this transformation—or conformation—will occur. Surely it will be at least the kind of transformation that occurs in our lives when we see someone whose excellence inspires us to be more excellent. Read with interest about a great person of prayer, and you will find that you will gradually pray more and with greater fervency yourself. When we actually see Jesus and we ourselves are glorified, we will seek to be more like him than ever before.

But there must be more to the idea that "we shall be like him, for we shall see him as he is." Seeing Christ and being made like him must also refer to the end of the great process of sanctification and glorification that God works in believers' lives through the work of his Holy Spirit. Already in this world, we receive the Holy Spirit in our hearts as a downpayment on our inheritance of eternal life with God. But now the influence of the Holy Spirit within us is often compromised by our own lack of interest in what he is doing, to say nothing of the fierce temptations that distract us from doing God's holy will.

While we live in this world, believers' resemblance to their heavenly Father and their brother Jesus is vague and disfigured. But that will all change.

Believers in Christ have a glorious future. True, they have not yet seen Jesus, but someday they will. And when that happens, they are going to be changed so that they will be like him. What more could we ask?

Blessed Jesus, "you have bought us, thine we are." We thank you for providing us with a salvation that includes our ultimate transformation so that we will be like you. As we look into the future, help us rise above the sometimes dreadful events that occur in our lives as we remember that you are going to transform us wonderfully. We pray in your name, Amen.

Meditation 98

His Glory and Ours

"I want [them] . . . to see my glory."
John 17:24

When they prep us and wheel us toward the operating room, we have just one thing on our minds. What's the operation going to be like? Will we survive? We think only of ourselves.

Jesus was different. The apostle John's gospel carefully records Jesus' actions and words on the way to the cross (see John 13-19). First there was the holy meal and then Jesus and the disciples left the upper room and made their way across the Kidron Valley to an olive grove. At some point that evening Jesus told them about the coming of the Holy Spirit. It was also on that evening that he prayed his high-priestly prayer (John 17). At that point—in that prayer—he was thinking about glory, about his glory and mine.

Glory is what reality is all about. When you think of God before he created the universe, think of glory. Always when you think of God, think of glory. Beyond the brutal cross, Jesus saw glory ahead.

Thus, as he moved toward his darkest hour, his mind was overflowing with the idea of glory. We marvel that the Bible allows us to see the inner workings of Jesus' mind and heart here. What a grace it is to be able to listen to his prayer! We are flabbergasted to discover that he thought not only of himself and his glory but also of our glory—the glory of those who believed in him and those who would believe in him in the centuries ahead.

"Father," he prayed, "I want them to be with me, and I want them to see the very same glory you gave me because you loved me before the creation of the world" (see 17:24). Jesus was thinking of us as he went to the cross. That's incredibly wonderful. And he didn't just ask his Father to take care of us somehow or another in his absence, but he told his Father that he wanted us to be right there when the victory was won and his glory would be revealed.

It's marvelous to remember that we have been created to share Jesus' glory throughout all eternity. Elsewhere the Bible tells us that Jesus endured the cross because of the joy he saw ahead of him. What was that joy? It was his glory. And that glory includes us who believe in him. The joy he saw was not just a luminescent brilliance far ahead; it was a glory that involved you and me. God the Father, the Son, and the Holy Spirit apparently want to spend eternity with us, and now they are filled with pleasure as they contemplate the joy there will be when all of us, billions strong, are with them forever.

While we live in this sometimes sordid world, we keep striving for glory. We want to rise above the tawdry, the ordinary, the commonplace, and the mundane. This is why we try to keep our houses looking decent—we decorate and redecorate and remodel. We go on exotic vacations if we can scrape up enough money to do it. We take cruises. We are looking for glory. That's a leftover of our paradise nature. It's ingrained in us. We know that we were not created to live shabby lives; we are glorious imagebearers of God!

Yes, it's going happen. We will be with God, and we will see his glory, and when we see his glory, we are going to be like him. That's the way it will be. The apostle John said that when he wrote to the churches. We cannot see the glory of Jesus and stay looking like we always have looked in this world. When we see his glory, we will be glorified just as he was.

What a blessed Savior we have! What a great God we have! Father! Son! Holy Spirit! Look what they have done for us. Look what they are doing for us. Look at what they are going to do for us throughout all eternity. We will be glorified. Just think of it. And Jesus, our Savior, is going to be full of happiness because finally he and all the rest of us will be together. How God loves us!

I must never forget this. Never. Even when they wheel me to the operating room. What a joy it is to have such a Savior!

Holy Spirit, don't let me ever forget what Jesus prayed for as he went to the cross. Help me always to remember that what he did on the cross was enough to make it possible for me to be joyful, even when the circumstances of my life may be frightening. Help me eliminate anything from my life that is inappropriate for a person headed for glory. In Jesus' name, Amen.

These Blessed Dead

Their deeds will follow them.
Revelation 14:13

The splendor of the believers' journey on earth has something to do with the fact that they do heavenly deeds while in this world.

This idea puzzles us. On the one hand, there are so many things we've done that we want to forget forever. To contemplate spending eternity encumbered by our bitterness and lust—our wretched selfishness—is hideous beyond reckoning. We hope to be purged of all that.

On the other hand, we have been taught that even our best works are imperfect and polluted by sin. We have discovered the humbling accuracy of this harsh judgment. Our works are seriously flawed, and, if we examine motivations, we have to concede that often something unworthy lay at the root of our activity. And if, through flashes of insight, we have been able to see the truth of this for ourselves, we assume that even when we cannot see how unworthy our motivations are, they most likely are anyway.

So then, what works dog the footsteps of the blessed dead? "Their deeds will follow them," we read. It's as if they come into the presence of God like toddlers who drag their little blankets behind them.

It is probably impossible to identify even one of these deeds while we are on this splendid journey because the works we will drag behind us into glory are probably inadvertent. Inadvertent acts are things we do without realizing it. Someone may come to us ten years after something happened and say, "You helped me so much when I had cancer—you spoke to me, and just the way you said you cared lifted my heart. I shall never forget it."

The deeds that will follow us must be those works that God has prepared for us to do. In Ephesians 2 we read that intense religious works carried out to earn salvation are hurled onto the ash heap. But in the same paragraph we find that we have been saved for good works that God has prepared for us to do, even before we were saved.

The works that follow the blessed dead into glory are not a currency that can be applied to their debt; the works that follow them are part of the grace God supplies in saving us and giving us new life. In other words, God not only saves the blessed dead but he also has prepared a specific treasury of works for each of them to do during their lives. These works, which are amazing-grace gifts just as their salvation is, make their lives splendid in God's sight.

Even so, those works are inadvertent; they are done naturally by those whose natures are being transformed through the power of the Holy Spirit within them. Jesus describes the puzzlement of those who will discover on the day of judgment that they are credited with visiting Jesus and doing him kindness (Matt. 25:37-40). "When did we ever do that?" his followers will ask. "You did it when you didn't even realize it," he will say. "You did it when you were kind and loving, when you went out of your way to help someone."

Because of our various preoccupations and our ignorance, we are not usually able to discern the splendor of our earthly lives. But we are invited to believe they are splendid nonetheless. We believe they are splendid because we know that God is working in us. "It is no longer I who live, but Christ who lives in me" (Gal. 2:20, RSV).

In the prime of life, with tons of groceries to buy and diapers to change, we can remember this. And on the cusp of eternity, when our strength is gone and we wonder why we still remain this side of glory, we may believe that there is a splendor to our lives.

What will the works be that will follow me? No one can begin to answer that question while here, for those who try will surely be mistaken. One of the exciting things about the next life is that we will discover how this life was truly a preparation for the next, and we will see, for the first time, the works God gave us to do that shine with heavenly splendor.

O gracious God, thank you for saving us and for giving us splendid works to do. Thank you for energizing us with your loving presence. Humble us, O God, with the realization that in ourselves we can do nothing worth taking with us into heaven. But also fill us with great joy as we believe that in spite of ourselves, we can do works worthy of that glorious place. In Jesus' name, Amen.

Journey's End: The Crystal Sea

Before the throne there was . . . a sea . . . clear as crystal.
Revelation 4:6

When Janaya was three years old, she could sing all three stanzas of "By the Sea of Crystal." If we asked her to do it, she wouldn't; she was too shy (or stubborn?). But sometimes, when she didn't think we were listening, the song would come out of her little heart.

Her mother taught it to her at bedtime from infancy on; Janaya's mother would hold her by her crib and sing the song, and when it was finished, she would lay her down. When we adults listened to her sing it, we marveled that she knew all the words, but we realized that she really didn't understand them.

And then we realized that we didn't understand either.

The song is a powerful one, though little known in the Christian community. Its words are straight from the book of Revelation, and the music is dramatic: *"By the sea of crystal saints in glory stand, myriads in number, drawn from every land. Robed in white apparel, washed in Jesus' blood, they now reign in heaven with the Lamb of God."*

And then the second and third stanzas declare: *"Out of tribulation, death, and Satan's hand, they have been translated at the Lord's command. In their hands they're holding palms of victory. Hark! the jubilant chorus, shouts triumphantly: 'Unto God Almighty, sitting on the throne, and the Lamb, victorious, be the praise alone.' God has wrought salvation; he did wondrous things. Who shall not extol thee, holy King of kings!"*

Big words, big ideas—Janaya didn't know what she was singing about. Big words, big ideas—Joel doesn't know what he is singing about either.

Yes, the journey is a splendid one, not because each day is set like a jewel in precious metal but because it is already eternal life to know the only true God and his Son, Jesus Christ, whom he has sent. And it is a glorious journey because of the destination: the throne of God and of the Lamb by the crystal sea.

The book of Revelation abounds with figures of speech that help us think about the new day that is surely coming. Then candles will be obsolete, and so will the sun. God will be our light. Night will be forever banished. And there will be crystal and precious jewels and semi-precious stones. There the streets will be of gold, and there won't be any potholes.

Janaya, little girl, let this man stand beside you and recognize that he has no more understanding of what it will be like in eternity than do you. Just as you listen to us older people and wonder sometimes what we are talking about, so do we look across the Jordan and wonder what it will possibly mean finally to be fully alive on the other side. Yes, there are words we can say and sing, like the words of "By the Sea of Crystal," but as we sing them, we realize we are trying to express realities that the vocabulary of earthlings can never grasp. Never.

That will be a new order of reality. Everything about it will be dominated by the presence of God. We shall see the person whom we have never seen but whom we love, though often so imperfectly—the Lord Jesus. We will discover a potentiality of being human that we cannot now imagine.

When three-year-olds hear their mothers sing of heaven, they believe their mothers. They do not realize that while their mothers sing, they pray that later in their children's day, when they are fifteen and twenty and beyond, they will still believe. And those for whom their mothers' songs are memories must realize that the crystal sea is there for them as they believe.

Today all we have is our faith. We have this life, ordinary, sometimes exasperating, occasionally terrifying, with its own goodness and happiness—we have this and we have faith. We believe. The faith has been given us; it's God's gift. When you have this life and faith in Christ, who shed his blood for your sin and who rose victorious from the dead and who is by the crystal sea right now, you know that someday you will be there with him.

By the sea of crystal. Janaya, what will that possibly be like?

O loving God, thank you for faith. What would we have to look forward to without faith? Thank you for sending Jesus, the Son of your love. Thank you, Jesus, for dying and paying the price. Thank you, Holy Spirit, for attending us and assuring us that we shall gather at the crystal sea. Thank you. Thank you. Thank you, O loving God. In the name of Jesus we pray, Amen.